New Recipes From your
RICE COOKER

Coleen and Bob Simmons

BRISTOL PUBLISHING ENTERPRISES
Hayward, California

A **nitty gritty**® cookbook

Printed in the United States of America.

ISBN 1-55867-301-6

Includes material revised from **The Versatile Rice Cooker** ©1996 Bristol Publishing Enterprises, Inc.

Cover design: Frank J. Paredes
Cover photography: Foodpix/Fiocca
Illustrations: James Balkovek

CONTENTS

A VERSATILE WAY TO COOK THE MOST VERSATILE FOOD

One half of the world's population eats rice at least once a day. For these people a rice cooker is the most sought-after kitchen appliance. Not only does it cook rice perfectly every time, but it will keep rice warm and delicious for several hours after cooking.

Because the cooker is always used for rice, usually cooked plain, other uses are rarely explored. The rice cooker makes a perfect vegetable steamer, and can be used to prepare a variety of delicious, healthful one-dish meals that can be served directly from the cooker. In addition we include several recipes that start with cooked rice for a base and some old favorite recipes that are served over cooked rice. Dim sum, the delightful Chinese snacks, can be easily made ahead and steamed in the rice cooker just before serving.

The rice cooker is a handy appliance for the home kitchen, the dorm room or studio apartment, the kitchen remodel or the ski cabin. It is an all-purpose pot. Consider using it to cook frozen vegetables or entrées in pouches, or to steam fresh vegetables, fish or chicken. Cook pasta for two, drain, and then add the sauce and allow it to heat through. It also can be used as a stew or soup pot, or for making risotto. It is much faster to reheat foods in the rice cooker by steaming rather than using an oven.

ABOUT RICE COOKERS

With such a large and diverse market it stands to reason that there would be many brands, styles and models of rice cookers to select from, starting with small, basic "on-off" or "cook-hold" models through large, expensive computer-controlled models for domestic use, and also very large models for restaurants. All will produce perfectly cooked rice if properly used.

All "on-off" or "cook-hold" rice cookers work on the same principle. An inner pan sits on a heated plate that brings water in the pan to a boil. The water boils vigorously until it is absorbed by the food, or boils off as steam. A temperature sensor in contact with the pan feels the rise in temperature above that of boiling water and reduces the heat to "warm," which keeps the contents of the pan at the proper serving temperature without burning.

The advantage of the more expensive computer-controlled rice cookers is in their ability to cook a wider variety of rices and also to provide the soak period desirable in producing a fluffy, individual grained rice for pilafs or rice salads. Because they have a computerized "mind" of their own, they are not as adaptable for steaming and cooking a variety of dishes based on grains or other ingredients.

To test these recipes we used a basic large (8 to 10 cup) "cook-hold" cooker. The model we used had the very desirable nonstick removable pan, which makes cleanup a breeze. Another nice feature was a plastic steamer insert that fits down into the cooker pan. It is quite simple to devise a method to turn any basic rice cooker into a steamer.

RICE COOKER ACCESSORIES

The rice cooker usually comes with a small flat steamer rack or plate, a rice measuring cup and sometimes a flat rice serving spoon. There are several other accessories that will make rice cooker recipes even easier. You may already have some of these items in your kitchen.

It is very desirable to have a collapsible stainless steel or plastic steamer basket. Buy one that fits easily into your cooker. Farberware makes a 9-inch black plastic one that works well. It has a detachable plastic handle that stays relatively cool when steaming.

A long-handled plastic spoon is very handy to have when using the rice cooker. Long-handled to keep your hands away from the steam and hot sides of the cooker when stirring or dishing up, and plastic so as not to scratch the finish in the bottom of the pan. This spoon is also handy for scraping rice grains from the bottom of the pan during cleanup.

Many rice cookers come with a 2½ or 3-inch high plastic basket that sits into the top of the rice cooker container. It is convenient to have a platform to hold a steamer plate 2 to 3 inches above the pan bottom. If yours doesn't have one, we made a serviceable one by cutting the top and bottom from an 8-ounce can that had contained crushed pineapple. There are also inexpensive platforms, made expressly for the purpose, available where woks and accessories are sold. Or use an artichoke holder made of stainless steel, which is also perfect for holding a plate during steaming.

Depending on the size of your cooker pan, you may find a bamboo steamer basket that will fit down about halfway into the cooker pan. The 8-inch size is perfect in a cooker that is about 9 inches across the top.

Bamboo steamer baskets can be stacked two or three high to steam individual plates of fish or chicken, and also make it possible to do larger quantities of dim sum or timbales. Use the bamboo lid on the top steamer. If necessary, wedge a clean dishtowel between the steamer basket and the rice cooker pan to prevent excessive loss of steam.

A plate lifter is very handy to help lift hot plates from the cooker or steamer baskets. Several varieties are available, and they are quite inexpensive.

HELPFUL HINTS

If your rice cooker pan is not coated with Teflon or another special slick surface, be sure to spray the rice cooker pan liberally with a high quality nonstick cooking spray. This will make cleanup much easier. The spray adds very little either in flavor or calories.

We use kosher salt in the rice cooker. It has no impurities or additives and dissolves easily. **You will need to use about half again more kosher salt than you would table salt.**

Measuring cups that come with various brands of cookers differ somewhat in size but they are usually about 6 fluid ounces. We assume that they are meant to be about the amount of rice for 1 portion. Please note that all our measurements are given in standard 8 oz. cups.

If the rice cooker shuts off before the food is totally cooked, add more water and start the cooker again.

The best way to clean the cooker pan is to fill it with warm soapy water and allow it to soak for a few minutes, and then use a plastic spoon or scrubber to loosen any adhering rice. Cooked rice does not come off in well in the dishwasher, and over time the dishwasher detergent will harm the hard anodized coating that is on some cooker pans. The new nonstick-lined pans clean very easily by hand.

Unlike most appliances, many rice cookers do not have an "on-off" switch, and must be unplugged to be totally off. Many have a pilot lamp to warn you that they are still on, but always remember to unplug the cooker after you have removed the food from it.

SAFETY CONSIDERATIONS

As with any appliance, there are things that one should keep constantly in mind.

1. When lifting a detachable cover, always lift it away from your face and arms. Steam can cause serious burns. Hinged covers will spring open at the touch of a button and it is important to avert your face and quickly move your hands to avoid the steam.

2. Don't allow the cooker cord to hang over the counter edge. A child could pull it off, or even brushing with an apron could pull a boiling pot off onto your feet and cause a serious burn.

3. Some rice cookers have an on-off switch, but most only have two states, cook and warm. After cooking, the appliance switches to warm and will keep cooked rice in perfect condition for serving for an hour or two. This is fine because plain cooked rice is not a good medium for bacterial growth. If, however, you cook other ingredients, especially chicken or seafood with the rice, the contents of the cooker should be removed immediately after cooking to assure that no harmful bacteria multiply.

4. While not exactly a safety consideration, we discovered the hard way that it is unwise to dispose of large quantities of cooked rice down the kitchen sink. The rice will eventually create a barrier that will defy drain cleaners. The best way to clean your cooker pan is to fill it with hot water and allow it to soak for a few minutes. Then scrape the grains that inevitably stick to the bottom of the pan with a plastic scraper or spoon. Pour the water through a strainer to catch the rice, and empty the strainer into the trash.

CHINESE RESTAURANT-STYLE RICE

The Chinese prefer rice that is not as sticky as Japanese rice but they still want a rice that is easily eaten with chopsticks. Chinese restaurants often cook a blend of rices, which is a mixture of long-grain, medium-grain and jasmine rices. The long-grain is for texture, the jasmine provides fragrance, and the medium-grain holds the cooked rice together so that it may be more easily eaten with chopsticks. Chinese restaurants rarely salt steamed rice while it cooks. The rice serves as a foil for the savory, salty dishes that are served with it. A blend that works well for us is:

½ cup long-grain rice
¼ cup jasmine rice
¼ cup medium-grain rice

Add rice to cooker pan and wash well in three or four changes of water. Then drain well. Add 1¾ cup cooking water and salt if desired. If you have time, allow rice to soak for 15 minutes before turning on cooker. When cooker shuts off, fluff up the rice with a fork, replace cover, and allow rice to steam for 10 minutes before serving.

BASIC INGREDIENTS TO USE WITH THE RICE COOKER

LONG-GRAIN RICE

Carolina—No longer from the Carolinas, but grown in Texas, Louisiana, Arkansas and Missouri. It cooks up with firm individual grains and has a pleasant neutral taste. Mahatma is a commonly available brand.

Jasmine—From Thailand. Aromatic, but doesn't smell of flowers. The aroma is described as "earthy" or "nutty," neither of which is a perfect descriptor. Has same appearance as long-grain. Cooks up soft and tender.

Indian basmati—Grown in the Himalayan foothills. True basmati has very long, slender grains that stay separate when cooked. It is intensely fragrant and has a wonderful aroma while cooking. Basmati is the perfect accompaniment for curry, and makes wonderful pilafs. The finest basmati rices are aged for a year or two after harvest to enhance the aroma.

Texmati, Jasmati and California "basmati"—All are hybrids, with some characteristic Jasmine or basmati aroma.

Parboiled—Widely available as "converted." Specially processed to retain more vitamins and nutrients. Requires more water, and a longer cooking time than regular long-grain rice. Cooked grains are firm and stay separate.

MEDIUM-GRAIN RICE

Medium-grain rice is sold under a variety of names. The grains are about twice as long as they are round. Medium-grain rice is bland and slightly stickier than long-grain. Medium-grain rice can be used in almost any recipe that calls for long-grain. Calrose is a widely available variety. In a pinch, Calrose will even make an acceptable risotto or paella.

Arborio rice—A very special medium-grain rice imported from Italy. Used for risotto in which it is cooked until just barely done in the center of the grain, and the surface starch creates a wonderful creamy sauce. It is possible to make a delicious risotto in the rice cooker. Valencia rice from Spain that is generally used in paella is very similar to Arborio, and the two can be used interchangeably.

SHORT-GRAIN RICE

Short-grain rice is also called "**pearl rice.**" Cooks up soft and sticky. This is the rice used to make sushi and rice pudding. Short-grain rice is not widely available except in Asian and Puerto Rican markets.

BROWN RICE

During the milling process, brown rice has a portion or all of the bran layer left on the rice grains. Nutritionally, brown rice has more B-complex vitamins and much more fiber than polished rice. Almost any rice type can have the bran left on the grain. The most popular brown rices are medium- and long-grain. Brown rice takes about three times as long to cook as polished rice, and the cooked rice retains a chewy texture. Since brown rice retains the germ and natural oils, it can turn stale and rancid if stored at room temperature for an extended period. Buy only what you need for a month or two. Store in an airtight container in a cool dark place to preserve maximum freshness and flavor.

EXOTIC RICES AND BLENDS

Several rice producers market special hybrid rices and blends. One of our favorites is Konriko "Wild Pecan" rice. It is neither wild rice, nor does it contain pecans. It is hybrid rice specially processed to remove about 20 percent of the bran that allows it to cook in just slightly more time than polished rice. The flavor is nutty and delicious. Lundberg Farms markets several distinctive blends of rice. We particularly like their Wild Blend, which is a combination of brown, sweet Wehani and black Japonica varieties. There are many other specialty rices available, as well as spiced and flavored rice mixes. All cook well in the rice cooker. Follow the package cooking directions.

RICE STORAGE AND COOKING

White rice will keep indefinitely if stored in an airtight container in a dark, cool place. Brown rice has a limited storage life, so buy only a two or three month supply. Some people like very soft rice while others prefer individual gains with some resistance to the bite. The softness of rice cooked in the rice cooker can be controlled by the amount of water added. Start out following package directions, and adjust the water to your taste. When the amount of rice is doubled, it isn't necessary to double the water. About two-thirds more is usually adequate. Salt the cooking water, if desired. About $\frac{1}{2}$ tsp. of salt for each cup of uncooked rice is a good starting place. If the rice is to be served plain, 1 tbs. of butter or olive oil added to the cooking water for each cup of rice will give the rice a nice silky texture and will keep the grains more separate. When the cooker shuts off, fluff up the rice with a fork and immediately replace the cooker cover. Allow to steam for 10 minutes more for perfect rice.

THE RICE COOKER PANTRY

Cooking in the rice cooker is fast, and if you have some of these basic pantry items, you can quickly put together a satisfying dinner.

NON-STICK COOKING SPRAY

There are many nonstick cooking sprays on the market. Names with wide market recognition are marketed as Pam, Mazola and Bertolli. There are many other vegetable and olive oil sprays available, and all do an excellent job, adding few calories. Spraying the rice cooker container with these sprays makes cleanup a much easier task, particularly because you don't want to use an abrasive scrubber on the special finishes of the rice cooking pan.

STOCKS AND BROTHS

A stock or broth adds flavor, improves texture and provides some nutritional benefits to recipes, particularly soups and dishes based on rice or grain. Dishes cooked in a rice cooker do not have the benefit of the long simmering or braising that it takes to develop a flavorful broth. The best stocks are homemade but if none are available there are many products in the supermarket that provide most of the benefits of homemade stock or broth. They are concentrated and ready to use, and come in a variety of flavors, in bottles, cans, cubes, and granules. Perhaps the most satisfactory products are sold in cans, often containing a little less than 2 cups of broth, just the right amount needed to cook 1 cup of rice. Chicken, beef and vegetable broths are the most commonly available. Alternatively, clam juice can be used and is usually available in a bottle or can. One of these products can be used for some or all of the liquid in most recipes .

Also available are bouillon cubes in a wide variety of flavors. One cube and 1 cup of water usually makes 1 cup of stock. The cubes can be added to the rice cooker with the water. There is no need to dissolve them first. These cubes have a long shelf life, and you need only open the exact amount you need. Reconstitute flavored cubes, bases, and granules using the amount of product and liquid specified on the package directions.

There are "stock bases" or "soup bases" widely used by restaurants that are becoming increasingly available in supermarkets and discount warehouse stores.

Be aware that all of these products contain large amounts of sodium and should be used in moderation if this is a concern for your diet. Rice, however, is very bland and usually needs to be cooked or consumed with some salt to be palatable.

Reduced-sodium versions of stocks and broths are becoming increasingly available in most supermarkets and are good products. Use the product available to you that tastes good. If you have the time and inclination to occasionally make your own stock, by all means use it. You will be rewarded with better flavor and can control the level of sodium.

It is not necessary to seek out low-fat or fat-free stocks, particularly if there is going to be another fat, such as olive oil or butter, added to the recipe. The amount of fat in stock is small and it carries a lot of flavor.

OLIVE OILS

There is a wide range of olive oils available from Italy, Spain, France, Greece and California. They run the gamut in color from pale yellow to deep green, and from light and elegant to robust and full-flavored. Most of the rice salads and many other recipes in this book call for extra virgin or full-flavored olive oil because it adds another layer of aroma and taste. You will want to keep both extra virgin and virgin olive oils on hand.

Olive oils have a limited shelf life after opening, so buy only the amount that you will use in a reasonable time. Olive oil should be stored in a dark, cool place, but not in the refrigerator.

PACKAGED AND CANNED POULTRY, MEAT, SEAFOOD, & CHEESE

A large variety of high-quality products are available that can be stored at room temperature until being added to rice to make an interesting main dish. Consider buying these items for the pantry shelf:

Poultry: chicken and turkey in cans or foil pouches.

Meat: cooked real bacon bits in jars or packages, ham and roast beef in cans.

Seafood: tuna in cans or pouches, cans of crab, shrimp, or clams.

Cheese: Grated Parmesan or American cheese in cans.

CANNED TOMATO PIECES

There is a short period of a couple of months in the summer when tomatoes are at their tastiest. By all means, use ripe, fresh tomatoes if you have them. The Italian or plum tomatoes are now available year-round and are a good choice if you must have fresh tomatoes after the season. For the rest of the year, and for recipes that call for long cooking, substitute canned tomatoes. These are processed at their peak of perfection and outshine the tasteless, hard product found in the market after prime season. Italian-style canned tomatoes, usually Romanos, are fleshy plum shaped tomatoes with few seeds. Prepare these by cutting out the hard stems, and squeezing out the seeds, using a strainer to catch the seeds and pass through the juice. Discard the seeds, chop the tomatoes and add them with their juice to the recipe.

One of the handiest tomato products on the market is canned, ready-cut tomato pieces that are diced and packed in juice. The ratio of tomato to juice is high and we recommend using them for most of these recipes because they make a good substitute for fresh tomatoes without the peeling, seeding and dicing.

DEHYDRATED AND FREEZE-DRIED VEGETABLES

In these busy days when it is important to save time and still prepare nutritious foods for quick dinners, the dehydrated and freeze-dried vegetables available on the spice shelves of your supermarket can be tremendous time savers. They are high quality, and they make a satisfactory substitute for fresh items after they have been boiled for a few minutes in liquid. However, if you have time and fresh vegetables on hand, do use them.

ONIONS

Peeling and cutting up onions isn't anyone's favorite job. Because most of the rice preparations cook for at least 15 minutes, dehydrated onion can be used when onion is called for in the recipe. Nationally known manufacturers, such as Schilling and Spice Islands, produce excellent dehydrated onion flakes.

Freeze-dried granulated garlic is another item handy to have on the pantry shelf.

CELERY FLAKES

How many times have you purchased a bunch of celery and used 2 or 3 stalks, storing the rest in the vegetable drawer until it is over the hill? A teaspoon or tablespoon of dried celery flakes adds celery flavor without the necessity of browning the fresh product in fat to soften it before adding to a recipe.

CHIVES

Freeze-dried chives are one of the better freeze-dried herbs. Fresh chives are becoming more available year-round in the market, but the dried product has great texture and taste. Substitute them for fresh in any dish.

PARSLEY

Flat-leaf (Italian) parsley has a stronger flavor than curly-leaf parsley. Dried parsley has a weedy aroma. It doubles nicely for fresh when you don't feel like washing and mincing the fresh. It takes only seconds to reconstitute in a little liquid.

MUSHROOMS

Dried mushroom slices or pieces give dishes a savory mushroom flavor. These include the intensely flavored Italian porcini and the Asian shiitake. Both must be soaked before adding to a dish. Use the strained soaking water in the recipe for a more intense mushroom flavor.

NO STOVE, NO REFRIGERATOR, NO PROBLEM

Everyone needs some fast, delicious dishes that can be done with a minimum of chopping and cooking. In this chapter you will find recipes for the times when you have minimum cooking conveniences: for the dorm room; for the ski cabin; for when the kitchen is being remodeled. These savory recipes are done completely in the rice cooker.

Note: If your rice cooker doesn't have a nonstick cooking container, be sure to spray the container with nonstick spray before cooking for easy cleanup.

SAN ANTONIO RICE

Stir a jar of your favorite fresh salsa into the rice cooker, add rice and some fresh corn kernels, and you have a flavorful supper or side dish for grilled chicken or fish.

1 cup uncooked long-grain rice
1 jar (12 oz.) fresh salsa, mild or hot
1 tbs. vegetable oil
1 cup fresh corn kernels or 1can (11 oz.)
  Mexicorn with juice
½ tsp. cumin
½ tsp. salt
freshly ground black pepper to taste
1¼ cups water
minced fresh cilantro for garnish, optional

Add all ingredients except cilantro to the rice cooker container, stir, cover and cook. When liquid has evaporated, open cooker, quickly stir and re-cover. Allow to steam for 8 to 10 minutes before serving. Spoon onto a serving dish, garnish with fresh cilantro and serve.

BROWN RICE AND GREEN CHILES

The combination of rice, green chiles and cheese has always been a family favorite. The brown rice adds a nice texture and flavor.

1 cup medium-grain brown rice
3 1/4 cups water
1 tbs. dried minced onion
1 tsp. kosher salt, or 3/4 tsp. regular salt
1 can (4 oz.) diced green chiles with liquid
3/4 cup grated sharp cheddar cheese
1 tomato, peeled, seeded, chopped
fresh cilantro for garnish, optional

Add rice, water, onion and salt to the rice cooker container. Cover and cook until rice cooker turns off. Taste a couple of kernels of rice to be sure they are tender. If not, add 1/4 cup water and continue to steam. When rice is cooked, quickly stir in green chiles, cheese and tomato pieces. Re-cover and allow to steam for 10 minutes. Spoon onto a serving dish, garnish with fresh cilantro and serve immediately.

GREEN CHILE AND CHICKEN RICE

All you need is a can opener for this quick main course.

1½ cups medium-grain rice, such as Calrose
3 cups chicken broth, see page 12
2 tbs. dried minced onion
½ tsp. kosher salt
1 can (10 oz.) chicken breast chunks with liquid
1 can (4 oz.) diced green chiles with liquid

Place all ingredients in the rice cooker container and stir. Cover and cook until rice cooker shuts off. Stir and serve immediately.

THAI-STYLE RICE

Make this rice to serve with spicy foods. The coconut milk adds flavor and richness.

1 cup long-grain Jasmine rice
2 cups canned coconut milk
¼ tsp. ground cardamom
½ tsp. ground coriander
¼ tsp. salt
ribbons of fresh basil leaves or cilantro leaves for
    garnish, optional

Add all ingredients to the rice cooker container except basil or cilantro. Cover and cook until rice cooker shuts off, about 20 minutes. Allow to stand 10 minutes before serving.

EASY RISOTTO

This basic risotto is cooked uncovered until the rice is creamy and the broth has been absorbed. Seafood, cooked chicken, mushrooms, dried or fresh herbs can be added, as you like.

2 tbs. unsalted butter
2 tbs. extra virgin olive oil
1/2 cup finely chopped white onion, or 1 tbs. dried minced onion
1 cup Arborio or medium-grain rice
1 tsp. grated lemon zest
1 tbs. lemon juice
3 1/4 cups chicken broth, see page 12
1/4 cup dry white wine or dry vermouth
1 pinch white pepper
1 tbs. dried parsley
1/2 cup grated Parmesan cheese
kosher salt and freshly ground black pepper to taste

Heat butter and olive oil in the rice cooker container. Add onion and sauté for 3 to 4 minutes, until softened. Add rice and continue to cook for 2 to 3 minutes, stirring, until rice becomes translucent. Add chicken broth, lemon juice, wine and pepper. Cook uncovered, without stirring, for about 15 minutes after liquid comes to a boil. Taste a grain of rice. If it is tender and does not have a hard center, the risotto is done. Stir in lemon zest, parsley, and Parmesan cheese and adjust seasonings. Turn off rice cooker and allow risotto to stand for 2 to 3 minutes before serving on plates or in a bowl.

Mushroom and sausage variation: Soak 2 dried Shiitake mushrooms in warm water for 10 minutes. Remove and discard stem and cut cap into small pieces. Add to rice with 1 cup chopped sausage (linguiça, smoked turkey or other fully cooked "ready to eat" sausage, cut into small pieces) and ¼ tsp. dried sage or thyme when adding the chicken broth.

Seafood variation: About 2 minutes before rice is done, add ¼ lb. small peeled, de-veined shrimp, ¼ lb. small scallops, and ½ tsp. dried or 2 tsp. chopped fresh tarragon and some lemon zest. Omit cheese.

SHRIMP WITH SAFFRON RICE

Servings: 2–3

Saffron is costly but it adds a unique flavor and color to rice. Turmeric can be substituted to produce the color if not the flavor. The rice is timed to cook for a few minutes, then the shrimp are added for the last few minutes of cooking. Do not allow rice to steam after rice cooker shuts off because shrimp will be overcooked. Jasmine rice is a good choice for this dish.

1 cup jasmine or long-grain rice
1 cup chicken broth, see page 12
1 bottle (8 oz.) clam juice, or 1 cup water
2 tbs. unsalted butter
1 tbs. dried minced onion
zest of 1 lemon
2 tbs. lemon juice

generous pinch saffron, or $1/4$ tsp. turmeric
5–6 drops Tabasco Sauce, or to taste
kosher salt and freshly ground black pepper
    to taste
8 oz. large shrimp, peeled, de-veined, tails
    left on
fresh or dried minced chives for garnish

Place all ingredients except shrimp and chives in the rice cooker container. After liquid starts to boil, cook rice for 10 minutes. Carefully open rice cooker and add shrimp on top of rice. Cover and continue to cook until rice cooker shuts off. Serve immediately and garnish with chives.

ORANGE RICE PILAF

This is a delicious accompaniment for almost any fish, chicken or pork dish.

2 tbs. unsalted butter
1/4 cup onion, finely chopped, or 1 tbs. dried onion flakes
grated zest of 1 orange
juice of 2 oranges plus enough chicken broth to make 1 3/4 cups liquid
1 cup long-grain rice
1/2 tsp. kosher salt
1/4 cup slivered toasted almonds for garnish

Add all ingredients to rice cooker container except toasted almonds. Cover and cook until liquid evaporates, about 20 minutes. Allow to stand for 10 minutes. Spoon into a serving bowl, top with toasted almonds and serve immediately.

PASTA FOR 2

If you are using an 8- or 10-cup capacity rice cooker, it is possible to heat enough water to properly cook a satisfying pasta dinner for 2 or 3 people. The smaller pasta shapes such as rigatoni, farfalle, or radiatore work best. There are many delicious prepared pasta sauces on market shelves, so choose one with your favorite ingredients.

10 cups water
2 tsp. kosher salt, or 1½ tsp. regular salt
5 oz. dried pasta

1¼ cups prepared pasta sauce, about 12 oz.
grated Parmesan cheese

Add water to the rice cooker container, cover, and heat until water comes to a full boil. Add salt and pasta. Cover until water returns to a boil and then uncover. Cook pasta according to package directions or about 8 to 9 minutes, until pasta is al dente. Carefully drain pasta into a strainer, reserving ½ cup of pasta cooking water. Add pasta sauce to rice cooker container with ¼ cup of the reserved pasta cooking water. Cook for 2 to 3 minutes, until sauce is heated through. Add drained pasta to sauce, adding a little more cooking water if sauce is too thick. Continue to cook for 1 to 2 minutes, until pasta and sauce are hot. Add 2 to 3 tbs. grated cheese. Serve immediately on plates or in bowls, and pass additional Parmesan cheese.

RISI E BISI (RICE WITH PEAS, HAM AND CHIVES)

Servings: 4

This traditional Italian dish is a tasty accompaniment to roast chicken and grilled fish. Double the recipe for serving as part of a buffet: spoon the cooked rice into radicchio cups or hollowed-out tomatoes and place on a platter.

2 tbs. unsalted butter
1¾ cups chicken broth, see page 12
1 cup long-grain rice
¼ cup dry white wine
2 tbs. dried minced onion
½ tsp. dried thyme, or 1 tsp. fresh thyme
 leaves

kosher salt and white pepper to taste
1½ cups frozen peas, rinsed with cold water
¼ cup diced smoked ham or prosciutto,
 optional
1 tsp. minced chives, dried or fresh
grated Parmesan cheese, optional

Melt butter in the rice cooker container. Add all ingredients except peas, ham, chives and Parmesan. Cover and allow to cook until rice cooker shuts off. Carefully open the cover and stir rice. Add peas, diced ham and chives. Cover and allow to steam for 10 minutes. Serve immediately with grated Parmesan cheese, if desired.

QUICK MUSHROOM HERB RICE

"Wild Pecan" rice has more pecan aroma than taste, and is a great Southern product. Substitute 1 cup long-grain brown rice for the Wild Pecan rice if not available.

2½ cups water
1 box (7 oz.) "Wild Pecan" rice
2 tbs. unsalted butter
1 can (4 oz.) mushroom slices and pieces with juice
2 tbs. dried parsley
1 tbs. dried celery flakes
1 tbs. dried minced onion
freshly ground black pepper to taste
1 tsp. kosher salt, or ¾ tsp. regular salt
several drops red pepper sauce, or to taste

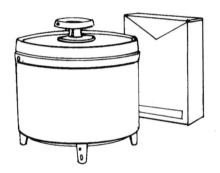

Pour water into the rice cooker container and add remaining ingredients; stir gently to combine. Cover and cook until rice cooker turns off. Carefully open lid, stir and replace cover. Allow to steam for 10 to 15 minutes before serving. Stir well and spoon into a serving dish. Serve immediately.

MADRAS CINNAMON SCENTED RICE WITH LENTILS

Servings: 3–4

The pretty pink colored dal, or split lentils, found in markets that sell ethnic foods, are combined with rice and spices for a tasty dish. If you have leftovers, use them to stuff hollowed-out fresh tomatoes, and steam for 5 minutes to heat through.

½ cup dal, picked over and washed
2 tbs. extra virgin olive oil
1 cup medium-grain rice
2½ cups vegetable or chicken broth, see
   page 12
2 tbs. dried minced onion
¼ tsp. granulated garlic
2 tbs. dried parsley

1 tsp. cinnamon
½ tsp. cumin
¼ tsp. crushed red pepper flakes
kosher salt and freshly ground black pepper
2 tomatoes, peeled, seeded, chopped, for
   garnish, or 1 cup drained canned tomato
   pieces
fresh cilantro for garnish, optional

Add all ingredients to the rice cooker container except tomatoes and cilantro garnish. Cover and cook until rice cooker shuts off. Carefully remove the cover, stir and re-cover. Allow to steam for another 10 minutes before serving. Place in a serving bowl, garnish with tomato and cilantro and serve immediately.

LEMON DILL RICE

This lemony rice is a delicious accompaniment for fish and chicken dishes. The lemon and herbs cook with the rice. Add shrimp or scallops and frozen peas during the last five minutes of cooking to make a main dish.

1 cup long-grain jasmine rice
1³/₄ cups water
¹/₂ tsp. salt
grated zest of 1 lemon
1 tbs. lemon juice
¹/₂ tsp. dried dill weed
1 tsp. dried parsley, or 1 tbs. minced fresh flat-leaf parsley
2 tbs. butter, cut into 4 pieces
kosher salt and freshly ground black pepper to taste

Add all ingredients to the rice cooker container. Stir to combine. Cover and cook until rice cooker shuts off. Allow rice to steam, covered, for 10 minutes. Adjust seasoning. Pour into a serving bowl and serve immediately.

SAVORY LENTILS

Lentils, like rice and pasta, provide a wonderful base for almost any combination of spices and flavors. This is a quick and easy side dish.

2 tbs. extra virgin olive oil
1/2 tsp. curry powder
1 tsp. cumin
1 cup brown or green lentils, picked over
   and washed
2 1/2 cups water

1 can (14 oz.) tomato pieces with juice
2 tbs. dried minced onion
1 tbs. dried vegetable flakes
2 tbs. dried parsley
kosher salt and freshly ground black pepper
   to taste

Heat olive oil in the rice cooker container and add curry powder and cumin. Cook for 2 to 3 minutes to bring out curry and cumin flavors. Add remaining ingredients, cover and cook until rice cooker shuts off. Midway through cooking, carefully open rice cooker and stir ingredients. Allow lentils to steam for 10 minutes before serving.

TUNA AND SPINACH RICE

Everyone has a favorite tuna and rice dish. Sprinkle with finely grated cheddar cheese just before serving, if you like that combination.

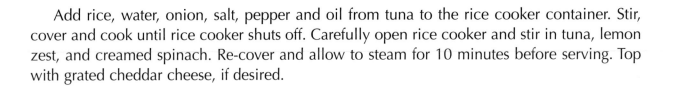

1 cup long-grain rice
2 cups water
1 tbs. dried minced onion
½ tsp. kosher salt
freshly ground black pepper to taste
1 can (6½ oz.) tuna packed in oil, drained, oil reserved
1 tsp. grated lemon zest
1 pkg. (10 oz.) creamed spinach, defrosted
cheddar cheese, optional

Add rice, water, onion, salt, pepper and oil from tuna to the rice cooker container. Stir, cover and cook until rice cooker shuts off. Carefully open rice cooker and stir in tuna, lemon zest, and creamed spinach. Re-cover and allow to steam for 10 minutes before serving. Top with grated cheddar cheese, if desired.

SALADS

The rice in salads tends to become a little dry in texture when refrigerated for several hours. Rice salads are best made and served the same day; however, they can be refrigerated, then allowed to come to room temperature with a little extra dressing added just before serving. Note: If your rice cooker doesn't have a nonstick cooking container, be sure to spray the container with nonstick spray before cooking, for easy cleanup.

TURKEY SAUSAGE BROWN RICE SALAD

Use low-fat smoked turkey sausage in this flavorful salad. Assemble the salad as soon as rice and sausage have cooled. While best when served an hour or two after being made, this salad keeps for 2 to 3 days in the refrigerator.

1 cup uncooked long-grain brown rice
2¼ cups water
1 tsp. dried minced onion, optional
½ cup diced smoked turkey sausage
⅓ cup coarsely grated carrot
2 tbs. finely chopped red onion
3 tbs. finely chopped celery

3 tbs. diced sweet pickle
2 tbs. minced fresh parsley
1 tbs. Dijon-style mustard
2 tbs. extra virgin olive oil
1 tbs. cider vinegar
kosher salt and freshly ground black pepper
    to taste

Add rice, water, onion flakes and smoked sausage to the rice cooker container. Cover and cook until liquid has evaporated, about 50 minutes. Check rice when steamer shuts off to see if grains are tender. If still a little crunchy, add 2 to 3 tbs. water, re-cover and continue to steam for another 10 to 15 minutes. Pour rice out on a shallow plate and allow to cool for a few minutes. When rice is barely warm, add remaining ingredients and mix well.

BASMATI RICE AND CORN SALAD

Domestically grown basmati does not need to be rinsed in several changes of water, but allowing it to soak for 15 minutes before cooking helps keep the grains separate when cooked.

1 cup basmati rice
1¾ cups water
¾ tsp. kosher salt, or ½ tsp. regular salt
2 cups fresh or frozen corn kernels
2 tbs. red wine vinegar
1 tbs. Dijon-style mustard

⅓ cup extra virgin olive oil
½ cup crumbled cooked bacon
5–6 green onions, white part with 1 inch of
   green, thinly sliced
kosher salt and freshly ground black pepper
2 tbs. chopped flat-leaf parsley for garnish

Add rice, water and salt to the rice cooker container. Soak rice for 15 minutes before turning on cooker. Cover and cook rice until cooker shuts off. Stir in corn, re-cover, and allow to steam for 10 minutes. Pour rice and corn into a large bowl and fluff mixture with a fork.

In a small bowl, whisk together vinegar and mustard, add olive oil and whisk well. Pour dressing over rice and toss gently to combine. Add bacon, green onions and salt and pepper to taste. Sprinkle parsley over salad just before serving. Serve at room temperature.

Variation: Substitute ⅔ cup toasted pecan pieces or slivered almonds for bacon.

PARTY RICE RING

When serving, try combining 2 cups cooked chicken cubes with ½ cup Italian-Style Tuna Mayonnaise. *Fill center of rice ring and garnish with olives and strips of roasted red pepper.*

1 cup long-grain rice
1 cup chicken broth, see page 12
1 cup water
2 tbs. extra virgin olive oil
2 tbs. sherry or rice wine vinegar
1 tsp. lemon juice
grated zest of 1 lemon

¼ cup chopped black kalamata olives
¼ cup diced pimiento or roasted red pepper
¼ cup coarsely grated carrot
3 to 4 green onions, white part with 1 inch
  of green, finely chopped
2 tbs. minced fresh flat-leaf parsley
kosher salt and freshly ground black pepper

Add rice, chicken broth and water to rice cooker container. Cover and cook until rice cooker turns off, then allow rice to steam for 5 to 10 minutes. Pour cooked rice into a large mixing bowl and fluff with a fork. Immediately toss with olive oil to keep rice grains from sticking together. Allow to cool for a few minutes. Stir in vinegar, lemon juice and lemon zest. Add remaining ingredients. Spray a 4- to 5-cup mold with nonstick spray. Press rice mixture into mold. Cover and let stand in a cool place for 1 to 2 hours to develop flavors. To release from mold, place serving plate over mold and invert. Serve at room temperature.

ITALIAN-STYLE TUNA MAYONNAISE

This makes a creamy sauce perfect for dressing cooked chicken cubes to serve in Party Rice Ring, *page 36. It is also delicious on* Steamed Turkey Tenderloins, *page 78, or drizzled over a platter of thinly-sliced cooked pork or veal, or to accompany sliced new potatoes or green beans. Italian-style tuna fish packed in olive oil is worth seeking out for its intense tuna flavor.*

1 large egg
2 tbs. lemon juice
1/2 tsp. salt
1 dash Tabasco Sauce
1 cup olive oil

1 can (6 1/2 oz.) tuna with oil
4 flat anchovies, rinsed and chopped
generous amount finely ground white
  pepper

Place egg, lemon juice, salt and Tabasco in a blender container or food processor bowl; process 30 to 45 seconds. At low speed slowly pour in oil. When mixture starts to thicken, add tuna with its oil, anchovies and white pepper; process until smooth. Refrigerate until ready to serve.

CURRIED RICE AND CHICKEN SALAD

This makes a great luncheon dish. Arrange the beautiful orange-hued rice on a platter, top with Basic Steamed Chicken Breasts, *page 70, and fresh cilantro leaves. Serve with* Cucumber Raita, *page 39.*

2 tbs. unsalted butter
1 tsp. curry powder
1 tsp. dried minced onion
1 cup basmati or long-grain rice
2 cups chicken broth, see page 12
$\frac{1}{2}$ tsp. cumin
$\frac{1}{4}$ tsp. dried dill
kosher salt
$\frac{1}{4}$ cup raisins, golden or dark
2 cups cooked chicken, cut into 1-inch pieces
$\frac{1}{3}$ cup coarsely chopped, unsalted dry-roasted peanuts
minced fresh cilantro leaves for garnish

Melt butter in the rice cooker container. Add curry powder and cook for 1 to 2 minutes to bring out flavor. Add onion flakes and rice; stir to coat rice. Add chicken broth, cumin, dill and salt. Cover and cook for 10 minutes. Add raisins, cover and continue to cook until rice cooker shuts off. Allow rice to steam for 10 minutes before removing cover.

Pour cooked rice onto a serving platter or bowl, and allow to cool for a few minutes. When rice is barely warm, arrange chicken pieces over rice and spoon a little *Cucumber Raita* over chicken. Sprinkle with peanuts and fresh cilantro leaves. Serve at room temperature with more *Cucumber Raita* and a chutney, if desired.

CUCUMBER RAITA

2 cups peeled, seeded, coarsely grated
  cucumber
1 cup plain yogurt
2 tsp. ground cumin

1 tsp. kosher salt, or $3/4$ tsp. regular salt
freshly ground black pepper to taste
$1/4$ cup chopped fresh cilantro or basil leaves
1 tbs. freshly chopped mint leaves

Combine ingredients in a small bowl. Cover and refrigerate for 1 to 2 hours before serving.

DELI RICE SALAD

Make this salad 1 to 2 hours before serving so flavors have time to marry. This is a great lunch or picnic treat. It assembles quickly with cooked rice and pick-up items from the deli.

2 cups cooked long-grain rice
1/2 cup drained and rinsed kidney or
   garbanzo beans
4 oz. salami or smoked ham, cut in slivers
4 oz. smoked Gouda or Provolone, cut in
   small dice

2 tbs. finely chopped red onion
1 medium dill pickle, finely chopped
2 tbs. finely chopped fresh flat-leaf parsley
1/4 tsp. crushed red pepper flakes
kosher salt and freshly ground black pepper
   to taste

VINAIGRETTE

1/4 cup extra virgin olive oil
2 tbs. cider vinegar
1 tbs. Dijon-style mustard

1/4 tsp. dried oregano
1/4 tsp. dried basil
kosher salt and freshly ground black pepper

Combine salad ingredients in a large bowl. Whisk vinaigrette until well combined, pour over salad and toss using two forks. If refrigerating, bring to room temperature before serving.

SAN JUAN BLACK BEAN AND RICE SALAD

Servings: 4

This hearty salad includes flavors of the Caribbean. If queso fresco (Mexican style fresh cheese) is not available, crumbled feta is a nonauthentic but delicious substitute. Serve with a fresh fruit platter of melon, mango and pineapple slices.

2 cups cooked medium-grain rice
1 can (15 oz.) black beans, drained and
   rinsed
1/4 cup diced roasted red peppers

6–8 black kalamata olives, pitted and
   chopped
3 oz. queso fresco or feta cheese, crumbled
minced fresh cilantro leaves for garnish

DRESSING

1/4 cup extra virgin olive oil
1 tbs. red wine vinegar
1 tbs. lemon juice

1 tbs. Dijon-style mustard
kosher salt and generous amounts freshly
   ground black pepper to taste

Place rice, beans, red peppers and olive pieces in a serving bowl and stir to combine. Whisk dressing ingredients together in a small bowl and toss with rice. Sprinkle with cheese and fresh cilantro. Serve at room temperature.

BUTTERNUT SQUASH AND RED PEPPER SALAD

Servings: 4

Together, the orange squash and red pepper make a colorful and healthful salad. Start with Steamed Butternut Squash, page 90, and pour the dressing over the squash while still warm.

1 lb. cooked butternut squash, cut into
   1-inch pieces
2 tbs. extra virgin olive oil
2 tbs. seasoned rice wine vinegar
1 tsp. Dijon-style mustard
1/2 tsp. kosher salt

1 pinch cayenne pepper
1 large roasted red pepper, cut into 1-inch
   squares
1/3 cup minced red onion
2 tbs. chopped fresh flat-leaf parsley
generous grinding black pepper

Place warm cooked squash in a medium bowl. In a small bowl whisk together olive oil, wine vinegar, mustard, salt and cayenne pepper and pour over warm squash. Gently toss to combine and allow to cool to room temperature. Add red pepper, onion and parsley and combine. Season with black pepper. Serve at room temperature.

MIDDLE EASTERN-STYLE KASHA SALAD

Servings: 6

Look for roasted buckwheat kasha to make this salad. Kasha has a nutty flavor and is very nutritious. Start draining the cucumber while the kasha is cooking.

2 cups chicken broth, see page 12
1 cup roasted kasha
1 cup peeled, seeded, diced cucumber
1/3 cup minced red onion
2 tbs. chopped cilantro leaves
2 tbs. chopped mint leaves
2 large tomatoes, peeled, seeded, chopped

VINAIGRETTE
2 tbs. extra virgin olive oil
2 tbs. red wine vinegar
1/2 tsp. dried oregano
1/2 tsp. dried basil
kosher salt and freshly ground black pepper
  to taste

To cook kasha: Pour chicken broth into the rice cooker container, cover and bring to a boil. Add kasha, cover and cook for 10 minutes. Turn off cooker and carefully pour kasha into a large bowl. Allow kasha to cool until just barely warm. While kasha is cooking, place cucumber in a strainer and sprinkle with a little salt. Allow cucumber to drain for 15 minutes, rinse briefly under cold water and pat dry with paper towels. In a small bowl, whisk vinaigrette ingredients to combine. Pour over kasha. Add cucumber, onion, cilantro, mint and tomato pieces to bowl. Toss to combine. Serve at room temperature.

SOUPS FROM YOUR RICE COOKER

Here is a collection of soups that can be made in less than thirty minutes in the rice cooker. Use a food processor to shred or slice the vegetables, add some canned or homemade chicken broth, dried or fresh herbs, and you'll have a quick, satisfying lunch or first course.

GINGERED CARROT ORANGE SOUP

Fresh ginger spices up this dramatic orange soup. It can be served hot or cold, and freezes well. Use the food processor to make quick work of shredding carrots. Push the finished soup through a coarse strainer for an extra silky finish if serving cold. Serve in glass bowls or teacups.

2 tbs. unsalted butter
1 small onion, thinly sliced
1 lb.carrots, coarsely shredded
1 tsp. finely minced fresh ginger
1/8 tsp. crushed red pepper flakes

3 cups chicken broth, see page 12
1 tbs. grated orange zest
1 1/4 cups orange juice
kosher salt and finely ground white pepper
minced flat leaf parsley or chives for garnish

Turn on the rice cooker and add butter to the container. When butter is foaming, add onions, carrots and ginger. Cook, uncovered, for 5 to 6 minutes until vegetables soften, stirring occasionally. Add chicken broth and orange zest. Cover and cook for 20 minutes, until carrots and onions are very soft. Turn off cooker and allow to cool for a few minutes. Add orange juice to carrots and carefully transfer mixture in 2 or 3 small batches to a blender or food processor. Process until smooth. Return soup to rice cooker container and reheat before serving. If serving chilled, pour into a large bowl, cover and refrigerate for several hours.

BLACK AND WHITE BEAN SOUP

Serves: 6

This hearty soup has as many variations as there are kinds of beans. Diced cooked ham, chicken or any type of cooked sausage can be substituted for the Portuguese linguiça. Drain and discard the black bean juice as it will make the finished soup look murky.

1 tbs. extra virgin olive oil
½ cup finely chopped onion
½ tsp. sambal oelek (a mixture of chiles, brown sugar and salt) or chile paste with garlic
1 cup diced cooked linguiça
2 cups chicken broth, see page 12
1 can (15½ oz.) diced tomatoes with juice

1 can (15 oz.) small white or cannellini beans, with juice
1 can (15 oz.) black beans, drained, juice discarded
kosher salt and freshly ground black pepper
¼ cup chopped fresh cilantro or parsley for garnish

Heat oil in the rice cooker container and add onions and sausage. Cook, uncovered, for 2 to 3 minutes, stirring. Add chicken broth, tomatoes and sambal oelek. Cover and cook for 15 minutes. Add beans and continue to cook for 5 minutes. Turn cooker off. Adjust seasoning. Serve immediately in warmed soup bowls and garnish with cilantro.

Note: Crushed red pepper flakes can be substituted for the sambal oelek.

PASTA EN BRODO

This satisfying Italian soup can be done in 20 minutes and combines a rich- tasting beef or chicken broth with pasta. Use any small shaped pasta such as little shells, stars, riso—or try miniature dried tortellini. Serve as a first course, or with a sandwich for lunch.

4 cups beef broth, see page 12
1 tbs. dried vegetable flakes
1 tbs. tomato paste
$1/2$ cup small dried pasta shapes

Pour broth into the rice cooker container. Add vegetable flakes and tomato paste. Cover and bring broth to a boil. Add pasta to boiling broth and cook for 8 to 10 minutes, until pasta is tender. Serve immediately.

POTATO AND LEEK SOUP

This classic soup cooks quickly in the rice cooker. It can be served hot or used as the base to make a cold Vichyssoise.

2 large leeks, white part only, thinly sliced
2 tbs. unsalted butter
1 medium stalk celery, thinly sliced
2 large baking potatoes, about 10 oz. each, peeled, thinly sliced

4 cups chicken or vegetable broth, see page 12
½ tsp. kosher salt
ground white pepper to taste
minced chives or flat-leaf parsley for garnish

Place sliced leeks in a strainer and wash under running cold water to remove any sand. Pat dry on paper towels. Melt butter in the rice cooker container, add leeks and celery, and cook, uncovered, for 4 to 5 minutes, until vegetables soften. Stir occasionally. Add potatoes and chicken broth, then cover and cook for 20 minutes, until vegetables are tender. Turn off cooker and allow soup to cool for a few minutes. Transfer potato mixture in 2 or 3 small batches to a blender or food processor and process until smooth. Adjust seasoning. Serve soup hot in warmed soup bowls and garnish with chives or parsley.

Vichyssoise variation: Combine 2 cups of potato and leek soup with ½ cup heavy cream. Cover and chill for several hours. Serve cold, garnished with chives.

CLAM CHOWDER

Make a quick clam chowder lunch or supper with pantry shelf items. Don't forget crackers.

2 tbs. unsalted butter
$\frac{1}{2}$ cup finely chopped onions
1 cup diced potatoes, about $\frac{1}{2}$-inch dice
$\frac{1}{2}$ tsp. kosher salt
$\frac{1}{4}$ cup chopped cooked bacon pieces

3–4 drops Tabasco Sauce, or to taste
1 cup (8 oz.) clam juice
2 cans ($6\frac{1}{2}$ oz. each) chopped clams
1 can (15 oz.) cream-style corn
kosher salt and white pepper

Melt butter in the rice cooker container. Add onions and potatoes and cook uncovered for 5 to 6 minutes, stirring occasionally. Drain clam juice into a measuring cup. Reserve clams. Add clam juice and enough water to make 3 cups liquid. Add clam juice mixture to rice cooker, cover and cook for 10 minutes after liquid has come to a boil, until potatoes are tender. Add clams and corn and continue to cook for 5 to 6 minutes. Season to taste with salt and white pepper. Turn rice cooker off and serve soup immediately in warmed bowls.

To make a richer, creamier soup, add only 2 cups liquid while cooking and add 1 cup of cream or half-and-half when clams and corn are added to rice cooker container.

HEARTY MAIN COURSES

Beans, lentils or a little meat round out rice-based dishes to make delicious main courses. Lentils cook as well as rice in the rice cooker, but require a little more liquid and time. We include traditional recipes for *Jambalaya* and *Chicken Cacciatore* that are ladled over hot rice. *Quick Fried Rice* is made from cooked, cooled rice.

Note: If your rice cooker doesn't have a nonstick cooking container, be sure to spray the container with nonstick spray before cooking for easy cleanup. It is a good idea to pour some water into the cooker container immediately after you remove the dish from the rice cooker.

SAVORY SAUSAGE AND RICE

This is a favorite rainy night dinner. Serve with a crisp green salad, garlic bread, and a red zinfandel wine.

1 cup uncooked long-grain rice
1 pkg. (2 oz.) chicken noodle soup mix
3½ cups water
1 lb. mild or hot bulk sausage
1 cup chopped onion
1 fresh red or green pepper, peeled, diced

1 tbs. dried parsley, or 2 tbs. chopped fresh
   flat-leaf parsley
2 tomatoes, peeled, seeded, chopped
kosher salt and freshly ground black pepper
   to taste
grated Parmesan cheese

Add rice, chicken noodle soup mix and water to the rice cooker container. Cover and cook until rice cooker shuts off. While rice is cooking, brown sausage in a nonstick skillet, crumbling into small pieces as it cooks. Remove sausage to a strainer and drain. Return about 2 tbs. of the sausage drippings to skillet. Sauté onion and red pepper for 5 to 6 minutes, until soft but not browned. When rice cooker turns off, carefully remove cover and quickly stir in cooked meat, onion mixture, parsley and tomatoes. Cover and allow to steam for 10 minutes. Spoon into a warm serving bowl and serve immediately. Pass Parmesan cheese if desired.

BASQUE-STYLE RICE AND CLAMS

Serve with a crisp salad, or fill individual clam shells or au gratin dishes for a first course. Fresh clams make an attractive garnish but the dish is delicious without them.

2 cans (6½ oz. each) chopped clams with juice
1 bottle (8 oz.) clam juice
3 tbs. extra virgin olive oil
½ cup chopped onion
2 cloves garlic, minced
1 cup uncooked medium-grain rice
⅓ cup finely chopped fresh flat-leaf parsley
1 large tomato, peeled, seeded, chopped
1 pinch saffron threads, optional
¾ tsp. kosher salt, or ½ tsp. regular salt
6–8 fresh clams in shells, scrubbed, optional
1 dash red pepper flakes
½ cup diced cooked ham or frozen green peas

Drain clams and strain juice through a coffee filter or cheesecloth to catch any sand. Reserve juice. Combine reserved clam juice with bottle of clam juice, plus enough water to make 2¼ cups total liquid. Heat olive oil in rice cooker container. When hot, sauté onions and garlic over low heat for 3 to 4 minutes, to soften onion. Pour in clam juice with water, rice, onion, parsley, tomato, saffron, salt, fresh clams (if using) and red pepper flakes. Cover and cook until liquid evaporates and rice cooker turns off. Immediately lift lid, remove cooked clams in the shell, and quickly stir in chopped clams, ham or peas and red pepper strips. Cover and allow to steam for an additional 10 minutes. Serve immediately on warmed plates. Garnish with whole clams in shell.

Variation: To serve as a first course, fill individual ovenproof serving dishes with rice and clam mixture. Sprinkle with buttered fresh breadcrumbs or Parmesan cheese. Place under broiler for a few minutes to brown lightly. Makes 6 to 8 first course servings.

ARROZ CON POLLO

Servings: 4

Succulent morsels of chicken are cooked with rice and spices to make a delicious supper or hearty lunch. Dried herbs and vegetables make this dish quick to prepare.

6 boneless, skinless chicken thighs, cut into
   1-inch pieces
3 tbs. extra virgin olive oil
1 red bell pepper, peeled, seeded, chopped
1½ cups medium-grain rice
2 tbs. dried minced onion
1 tsp. granulated garlic
1 tbs. dried parsley

2 tsp. Spanish paprika
3 cups chicken broth, see page 12
1½ cups canned tomato pieces with juice
½ tsp. Tabasco Sauce
kosher salt and freshly ground black pepper
   to taste
1 pinch saffron, optional

Heat olive oil in rice cooker container and sauté chicken pieces for 2 to 3 minutes, until lightly browned. Add red pepper and rice, and stir to coat rice. Add remaining ingredients, stir, cover and cook until rice cooker shuts off. Carefully remove cover and stir rice. Re-cover and allow to steam for 10 minutes before serving on warmed plates.

RICE WITH LENTILS

Sun-dried tomatoes accent this hearty dish. The brown lentils take longer to cook than rice, so they are started a few minutes before adding rice. Serve with a fresh fruit or green salad, crisp cheese bread and a red zinfandel wine.

1/2 cup lentils, picked over and washed
2 tbs. extra virgin olive oil
3 cups beef or chicken broth, see page 12
2 tbs. dried minced onion
1/2 tsp. granulated garlic
2 tbs. dried parsley
1 cup medium-grain rice

1/2 tsp. kosher salt
1 tsp. ground cumin
1/4 tsp. crushed red pepper flakes
1/4 cup diced sun-dried tomatoes
1 medium-size tomato, peeled, seeded, chopped, for garnish
2 tbs. chopped fresh flat-leaf parsley

Add lentils, olive oil and broth to the rice cooker container. Cover and cook for 15 minutes. Add remaining ingredients, except tomato pieces and parsley, and continue to cook until rice cooker shuts off. Carefully remove cover, quickly stir and re-cover. Allow to steam for 10 minutes before serving. Spoon into a serving bowl and top with chopped tomato and parsley. Serve immediately.

CHICKEN CACCIATORE

Servings: 3–4

Serve over rice. This dish can be made ahead and refrigerated for serving the next day.

6 chicken thighs, skinned
flour seasoned with salt and pepper
3 tbs. extra virgin olive oil
1/2 lb. mushrooms, sliced
1/2 cup chopped onion
2 cloves garlic, minced
3 tomatoes, peeled, seeded, chopped
1/4 cup dry white wine or vermouth

2 tbs. brandy
1 tbs. Worcestershire sauce
1/2 tsp. each dried, or 2 tsp. each fresh,
   tarragon, thyme, oregano
1 tbs. dried parsley, or 1/4 cup chopped fresh
   flat-leaf parsley
1/2 tsp. grated lemon zest
kosher salt and freshly ground black pepper

Lightly coat chicken with salt, pepper and flour mixture. Heat olive oil in a large skillet and sauté chicken until lightly browned on both sides. Remove to a plate. Add mushrooms to skillet and cook for 3 to 4 minutes, until softened. Add onion and garlic and cook for 2 to 3 minutes. Return chicken to skillet and add remaining ingredients. Bring liquid to a boil, cover, and cook over low heat for 30 minutes. Turn chicken pieces once or twice during cooking. If sauce appears thin, remove chicken to a plate and cook sauce over high heat for 5 to 6 minutes to reduce and thicken slightly. Serve immediately over hot long-grain rice.

BEEF STROGANOFF

This classic Russian favorite is served over hot cooked rice. Make the meat sauce ahead and add sour cream just before reheating and serving.

4 tbs. unsalted butter, divided
1 lb. flank steak, cut into 1/3- x 2-inch strips
1/2 cup chopped onion
1 clove garlic, minced
1 large tomato, peeled, seeded, chopped, or
  1/2 cup chopped canned tomatoes

1 tbs. Worcestershire sauce
6–8 drops Tabasco Sauce
1/2 cup beef or chicken broth, see page 12
kosher salt and freshly ground black pepper
1/2 lb. mushrooms, sliced
1 cup sour cream

Heat 2 tbs. of the butter over medium-high heat in a large skillet. When foaming, add steak pieces and sauté for 3 to 4 minutes, until lightly browned. Add onion, garlic, tomato pieces, Worcestershire sauce, Tabasco, beef broth, salt and pepper. Cover and cook over low heat for 20 minutes, until meat is tender. In another skillet, heat remaining butter over medium high heat and sauté mushrooms until lightly browned. Just before serving, combine mushrooms and sour cream with meat mixture and heat through, but do not boil. Adjust seasoning. Serve immediately.

JAMBALAYA

This classic Louisiana dish has many variations and can be made with leftover cooked chicken or ham. A few shrimp tossed in during the last minutes of steaming are always welcome.

2 tbs. extra virgin olive oil
1 cup coarsely chopped onion
1 red bell pepper, peeled and diced
1 medium stalk celery, diced
1 cup uncooked long-grain rice
1¾ cups chicken broth, see page 12
1 can (14 oz.) tomato pieces with juice
1 tbs. tomato paste
½ tsp. dried thyme

¾ tsp. kosher salt, or ½ tsp. regular salt
freshly ground black pepper to taste
1 pinch powdered cloves
¼ tsp. prepared chili powder
1 tbs. dried parsley
6–8 drops Tabasco Sauce
⅓ cup diced ham
6 oz. smoked Polish sausage, cut into slices
6–8 medium shrimp, optional

Heat oil in the rice cooker container and sauté onion, pepper and celery for 3 to 4 minutes to soften. Add rice and stir to coat. Add remaining ingredients. Cover and cook, stirring once or twice, until rice cooker turns off. Allow jambalaya to steam for about 10 minutes before serving on warmed plates.

QUICK FRIED RICE

Cold cooked rice is a must for good fried rice. Basmati rice is particularly good in this dish. Roll rice clumps between your fingers to break them into individual grains. For variation, use leftover cooked asparagus or broccoli instead of peas.

3 tbs. vegetable oil

4 green onions, white part and 2 inches of green, thinly sliced

3 cups cold cooked rice, crumbled

2 large eggs, lightly beaten

1/2 cup diced cooked ham, chicken, sausage or shrimp

1/2 cup frozen green peas, rinsed with cold water

2 tbs. soy sauce

1 tsp. toasted sesame oil

1/8 tsp. ground white pepper

fresh chopped cilantro leaves for garnish

Heat vegetable oil in a wok or a large nonstick skillet. Sauté onions for 1 to 2 minutes to soften. Add crumbled rice and cook for 3 to 4 minutes over medium heat, stirring constantly. Make a well in middle of rice and pour in beaten eggs. When eggs start to set, stir into rice, breaking into small pieces. Add ham, peas, soy sauce and sesame oil. Season with pepper and continue to cook for 1 minute, until mixture is hot. Garnish with cilantro and serve in a warm bowl or on warm plates.

SEAFOOD

Shellfish and other seafoods need only the quickest cooking or steaming to bring out their delicious flavors. Shrimp and salmon steamed with aromatic flavorings assemble quickly and fit right in with today's healthful eating patterns.

A small artichoke holder or a platform made out of an 8-oz. can with both ends cut out of it makes a good spacer to hold a plate above the steaming water. For quick cleanup, be sure to spray the plate used for steaming with nonstick cooking spray before placing fish and marinade on it. If your rice cooker doesn't have a nonstick cooking container, be sure to spray container with nonstick spray before cooking for easy cleanup.

SHRIMP COOKED IN BEER

This is an easy dish for informal entertaining. If you have any shrimp left over, refrigerate and eat them for lunch the next day. Choose a pilsner or light beer for steaming liquid.

1 lb. medium-size shrimp in the shell
12 oz. pilsner or light beer
1 pinch crushed red pepper flakes
kosher salt

With scissors, cut shrimp shells down the back and pull off the legs. Lift out the dark vein with a toothpick and rinse with water. Place shrimp in rice cooker container and pour in enough beer to just cover shrimp. Add red pepper flakes and 1 pinch salt. Bring beer to a boil, uncovered. Stir once or twice. Shrimp are done when they turn a bright pink, about 3 to 4 minutes after beer comes to a boil. Immediately pour shrimp into a strainer and then into a serving bowl. Serve warm, cold or at room temperature with lots of napkins, a bowl for shells and *Aioli,* page 112, or cocktail sauce.

SALMON FILLETS IN WHITE WINE AND MUSTARD

Servings: 2

Salmon fillets steamed with white wine and dill make an elegant dinner for two. Serve with fresh sweet corn and a salad of tender greens.

2 salmon fillets, about 6–7 oz. each
1 tsp. Dijon-style mustard
2 tbs. dry white wine or dry vermouth
1/4 tsp. sugar

1/4 tsp. dried dill weed, or 1 tsp. chopped
   fresh dill
1 green onion, white part with 1 inch of
   green, thinly sliced

Make two aluminum foil boats, each just a little larger than the fillets. Rub salmon with mustard and place in foil boats. Combine white wine, sugar and dill. Pour over fish and top with thinly sliced onion. Spray steamer plate with nonstick spray. Place foil boats on steamer plate. Place a rack or steamer platform in the rice cooker container and add 1 cup water. Place plate in rice cooker. Cover and steam for about 10 minutes after water starts to boil. Check fish at 8 minutes. The fish is done when it flakes or feels firm to the touch. Do not overcook. Carefully lift plate out of cooker using a plate lifter. Remove salmon fillets from foil and serve on warm plates. Pour cooking juices over fish, if desired.

SALMON STEAMED IN GRAPE LEAVES

Servings: 2

Canned grape leaves make a flavorful wrapper for fish or chicken and help retain moisture.

2 skinless salmon fillets, 6–7 oz. each
kosher salt and freshly ground black pepper
   to taste
extra virgin olive oil

1 tsp. chopped fresh dill or thyme
2 lemon slices plus 2 slices for garnish
4–6 grape leaves in brine, rinsed with cold
   water and dried

If necessary, fold thin parts of fish under to make pieces more uniform in thickness. Season with salt and pepper. Drizzle with oil, sprinkle with dill and place 1 slice of lemon on top of each. Cut protruding stems from grape leaves and discard. Arrange 2 or 3 leaves together, overlapping them if needed. Place fish in middle of leaves and bring edges together to enclose fish completely. Place grape leaf packages on a steamer plate sprayed with nonstick spray. Place a rack or steamer platform in the rice cooker container and add 1 cup water. Place plate in rice cooker, cover and steam for about 10 minutes after water starts to boil, depending on size and thickness of fish. Start checking fish at 7 or 8 minutes by cutting a slit with a knife. The fish is done when it flakes or feels firm to the touch. Do not overcook. Carefully remove plate from the steamer with a plate lifter. Place fish packages on plates and allow diners to unwrap grape leaf, or remove grape leaves and present fish with slice of lemon on top.

SALMON WITH HOISIN SAUCE

Hoisin sauce is found in Asian markets and in the ethnic food section of most supermarkets.

2 skinless salmon fillets, about 6 to 7 oz.
  each
1 tsp. hoisin sauce
2 tsp. rice wine vinegar

$\frac{1}{2}$ tsp. toasted sesame oil
2 tsp. soy sauce
$\frac{1}{4}$ tsp. grated fresh ginger
3–4 fresh cilantro leaves

Make two aluminum foil boats, each just a little larger than fish fillets. If necessary, fold thin part of fish under to make a more uniform piece. Combine remaining ingredients except cilantro leaves and spread on the salmon pieces. Place each fillet in a foil boat and top with cilantro leaves. Spray steamer plate with nonstick spray, and place foil packages on plate. Add 1 cup water and small rack or platform to hold plate in rice cooker container. Place plate in rice cooker container, cover and cook for about 10 minutes after water starts to boil. Start checking fish at 7 or 8 minutes. The fish is done when it flakes or feels firm to the touch. Do not overcook. Carefully lift plate from rice cooker with a plate lifter. Remove fish from foil and place on warmed plates. Pour some cooking juices over, if desired, and serve. Garnish with fresh cilantro leaves.

CHINESE-STYLE STEAMED ROCK COD

Almost any firm-fleshed fish (like red snapper, sea bass or halibut fillets) can be used here.

2 rock cod fillets, about 4–6 oz. each
1 tbs. soy sauce
1/4 tsp. toasted sesame oil
1 small clove garlic, minced
1 tsp. fresh ginger, minced
1 pinch white pepper

1 tbs. rice wine vinegar
2 green onions, white part with 1 inch of
   green, slivered
5–6 slivered snow peas
fresh cilantro leaves

Choose a plate that will allow about 1/2-inch circulation around it in the rice cooker container. Spray plate with nonstick spray. Place 2 fish fillets on the plate. Fold thin parts of fish under to make more uniform pieces. Mix together soy sauce, sesame oil, garlic, ginger, white pepper and rice wine vinegar. Pour over fish fillets. Top with slivered onions and snow peas. Cover plate with plastic wrap. Add 1 cup water and small rack or platform to hold plate in rice cooker container. Place plate in rice cooker container, cover and steam for about 7 to 8 minutes after water has come to a boil. The fish is done when it flakes or feels firm to the touch. Do not overcook. Carefully remove plate from rice cooker with a plate lifter. Place fish on warmed serving plates. Garnish with fresh cilantro leaves. Serve immediately.

STEAMED SHRIMP DIJON

Shrimp only need a delicate marinade and 4 to 5 minutes steaming to make a perfect appetizer for two, or an entrée when served over steamed rice.

4 oz. small shrimp, peeled, de-veined (51–60 per pound)

MARINADE

1 tsp. dry sherry
1 tsp. extra virgin olive oil
1 tsp. Dijon-style mustard

1 tsp. lemon juice
1/4 tsp. dried tarragon

Combine marinade ingredients in a small bowl. Toss shrimp with marinade and let stand for 10 minutes. Spray plate with nonstick spray. Arrange marinated shrimp in a single layer on the plate and cover with plastic wrap. Add 1 1/2 cups water and a small rack or platform to hold plate in the rice cooker container. Cover rice cooker and bring to a boil. When water in cooker comes to a boil, using a plate lifter, carefully place plate on plate support. Cover rice cooker and steam for 3 to 4 minutes, until shrimp are pink and firm to the touch. Carefully remove plate with a plate lifter and remove plastic wrap. Serve immediately.

Variation: Substitute 4 oz. small scallops for the shrimp.

CANTONESE-STYLE STEAMED SHRIMP

This is a traditional-style soy sauce-based marinade. The lemon rind and juice give a little flavor boost. Makes a great appetizer for two or an individual entrée with some rice and a vegetable. Small scallops can be substituted for the shrimp.

4 oz. shrimp, peeled, de-veined (about 51–60 per lb.)

MARINADE

1 tsp. soy sauce

1 tsp. toasted sesame oil

1 tsp. lemon zest

1 tsp. lemon juice

2 green onions, white part with 1 inch of green, cut into long slivers

Mix marinade ingredients together and marinate shrimp for about 10 minutes. Spray a small plate with nonstick spray and place marinated shrimp in single layer on plate. Cover with plastic wrap. Add 1½ cups water and small rack or platform to hold plate in rice cooker container. Cover rice cooker and bring to a boil. When water comes to a boil, using a plate lifter, carefully place plate on plate support. Cover and steam for 3 to 4 minutes, until shrimp are pink and firm. Carefully remove plate from cooker with plate lifter, remove plastic wrap and serve immediately as an appetizer or entrée.

STEAMED CLAMS

Allow an hour or so to soak the clams so they can release any sand. These are delicious served with some of the broth or a little melted butter and lemon juice for dipping.

1½ lbs. littleneck or cherry stone clams in the shell
1 tbs. kosher or sea salt
1 cup dry white wine or water

Wash clams under running water and place in a bowl covered with 1 quart of cold water and kosher salt. Allow to stand for an hour so clams release their sand. Drain and rinse clams. Place clams in a steamer basket and place basket in the rice cooker container with 1 cup wine or water. Cover and cook for 8 to 10 minutes after water starts boiling, until clams have opened. Remove opened clams to a bowl. Discard any clams that do not open. If desired, continue to cook broth for 3 to 4 minutes to reduce. Carefully pour off broth, leaving any sand in bottom of container. Serve broth in small bowls and use for a dipping sauce.

POULTRY

Boneless pieces of chicken or turkey steam quickly in the rice cooker. To set up the rice cooker for steaming, place a small rack or 8 oz. can with both ends cut out to make a plate platform. Choose a plate that will fit into the rice cooker with about $\frac{1}{2}$-inch clearance for steam circulation and spray with nonstick spray. Just add some aromatic herbs, wine or broth to a chicken and you have a healthful entrée. Pesto, mustard or the Asian combination of soy sauce and ginger all complement poultry.

BASIC STEAMED CHICKEN BREASTS

This basic steamed chicken breast recipe is great for salads and sandwiches. It is also good in soups.

2 boneless, skinless chicken breasts
kosher salt and freshly ground black pepper to taste

Choose a plate that is just large enough to fit into the rice cooker container with about $\frac{1}{2}$-inch clearance for steam circulation. Spray plate with nonstick spray. Place chicken breasts on plate and season with salt and pepper. Cover with plastic wrap.

Add 1 cup water to rice cooker container and in it place a small rack or 8 oz. can with both ends cut out to make a platform. Place plate on rack, cover rice cooker and bring water to a boil. Steam chicken for about 10 minutes after water has come to a boil, until chicken is firm to touch. Carefully remove plate from rice cooker container with a plate lifter.

SOY SAUCE-MARINATED CHICKEN BREASTS

Boneless, skinless chicken breasts or turkey cutlets are marinated and cooked in an Asian flavored sauce.

2 boneless, skinless chicken breasts or turkey breast cutlets, about ¾-inch thick
2 tbs. soy sauce
1 tbs. sugar
1 tsp. toasted sesame oil
1 small clove garlic, minced
½ tsp. grated fresh ginger
1 green onion, white part with 1 inch of green, cut into slivers

Combine soy sauce, sugar, sesame oil, garlic and ginger with chicken breasts and marinate for 10 to 15 minutes. Place chicken breasts and marinade on a plate sprayed with nonstick cooking spray, top with slivered onion, and cover plate with plastic wrap. Steam as directed for *Basic Steamed Chicken Breasts*, page 70.

Serve chicken breasts on plates with a spoonful of marinade.

CHICKEN BREASTS WITH WINE AND SHALLOTS

Boneless chicken breasts make a fast and savory dinner entrée.

2 boneless, skinless chicken breasts
2 tbs. unsalted butter
1 tbs. minced shallots
¼ cup dry white wine
kosher salt and freshly ground black pepper to taste
1 dash Tabasco Sauce
1 tomato, peeled, seeded, chopped
5–6 basil leaves, cut into thin shreds

Place boneless chicken breasts on a plate sprayed with nonstick cooking spray. In a small skillet, melt butter and sauté shallots for 1 to 2 minutes to soften. Pour in white wine, turn heat to high and reduce for 1 minute. Pour shallot mixture over chicken and cover with plastic wrap. Steam as directed for *Basic Steamed Chicken Breasts,* page 70. Remove chicken breasts to warmed plates and garnish with tomato pieces and shredded basil leaves.

CHICKEN BREASTS WITH PESTO

Homemade pesto or pesto from a squeeze-tube makes a zesty marinade for chicken breasts. Serve garnished with tomato, Parmesan cheese and toasted pine nuts.

2 boneless, skinless chicken breasts
1 tbs. pesto
kosher salt and freshly ground black pepper to taste
2 tbs. toasted pine nuts
1 tomato, peeled, seeded, chopped
grated Parmesan cheese for garnish

Place chicken breasts on a plate sprayed with nonstick spray. Spread pesto over top of breasts; season with salt and pepper. Cover plate with plastic wrap and steam as directed for *Basic Steamed Chicken Breasts,* page 70. Carefully remove plate from rice cooker with a plate lifter. Serve chicken breasts on warmed plates; garnish each serving with pine nuts, chopped tomato and a spoonful of Parmesan cheese. Serve immediately.

CHICKEN BREASTS DIJON

A simple marinade of Dijon-style mustard and yogurt makes a quick savory entrée. This makes a delicious hot toasted sandwich, as well. Chili bean paste with garlic can be substituted for the sambal oelek.

2 boneless, skinless chicken breasts
1 tbs. Dijon-style mustard
1 tbs. plain yogurt
½ tsp. sambal oelek (a mixture of chiles, brown sugar and salt), optional
kosher salt and freshly ground black pepper to taste
1 tsp. dried chives

Place chicken breasts on a plate sprayed with nonstick spray. Mix together mustard, yogurt, sambal oelek, salt and pepper. Spread over chicken breasts and sprinkle with chives. Cover chicken on plate with plastic wrap. Steam as directed for *Basic Steamed Chicken Breasts,* page 70. Carefully remove plate from rice cooker with a plate lifter and remove plastic wrap. Place chicken breasts on warmed serving plates. Serve immediately.

CHICKEN WITH ORANGE AND BLACK BEANS

Servings: 4

This spicy dish with refreshing flavors of orange, earthy black beans, and exotic garlic and ginger was inspired by a recipe of Ken Hom's. Dried salted black beans and sambal oelek are available in Asian markets and in the ethnic foods section of most supermarkets. Chili bean paste with garlic can be substituted for the sambal oelek.

1 tbs. vegetable oil
2 cloves garlic, minced
2 tbs. salted black beans, rinsed, chopped
1 tbs. fresh grated ginger
1 cup uncooked long-grain rice
grated zest of two oranges
1 cup orange juice

1 cup chicken broth, see page 12
3 tbs. soy sauce
$\frac{1}{2}$ tsp. sambal oelek, or substitute $\frac{1}{4}$ tsp. red pepper flakes or 6–8 drops Tabasco Sauce, or to taste
5–6 skinless, boneless chicken thighs, cut into 6–7 pieces each

Heat vegetable oil in the rice cooker container and add garlic, black beans and ginger. Cook, stirring, for 1 to 2 minutes, until garlic and black beans release some of their flavor. Add rice and stir to combine. Add remaining ingredients, cover and cook until rice cooker shuts off. Stir once during cooking. Allow rice to steam for about 10 minutes before serving.

CHICKEN SEAFOOD ROULADES

Chicken breasts are lightly flattened and spread with a creamy shrimp and scallop mousse, then rolled up and steamed. They make a delicious cold appetizer with red pepper or caper-flavored mayonnaise, or serve them hot with Clam Sauce, page 77.

3 boneless, skinless chicken breasts
1½ oz. small raw shrimp, peeled, de-veined
1½ oz. bay scallops, washed, white muscle removed
1 tbs. heavy cream

2 tsp. dried parsley, or 1 tbs. chopped fresh
1 tsp. dried or minced fresh chives
kosher salt and generous amount white pepper to taste

Place each chicken breast between 2 pieces of waxed paper. Starting in center, with a poultry or meat pounder, pound into an even flat thickness of about ½-inch. Place remaining ingredients in a food processor workbowl and process for 2 to 3 minutes, until very smooth. Spread seafood mixture over each chicken breast and roll into a sausage shape, about 2 inches in diameter. Tuck in sides as you roll to make a neat package. Wrap each breast in a double thickness of plastic wrap and tie ends of wrap with string. Place on a plate sprayed with nonstick spray.

Place a steamer rack or platform in the rice cooker and add 2 cups water. Place plate of chicken rolls on rack. Cover rice cooker, bring to a boil and steam for about 20 to 25 minutes. Rolls are done when firm to the touch. Carefully remove rolls from rice cooker. If serving hot, allow to cool for 1 to 2 minutes before unwrapping. If serving cold, leave in wrap and refrigerate for several hours or overnight before slicing and serving. To serve hot, slice each roll into 7 to 8 slices and slightly overlap them on individual plates. Spoon some *Clam Sauce* over chicken and serve.

To serve cold, after refrigerating cut into 8 to 10 slices, and place on crackers or small toasts with a dollop of flavored mayonnaise.

CLAM SAUCE

1 tbs. unsalted butter
4 green onions, white part with 1 inch of
    green, thinly sliced
8 oz. clam juice

kosher salt and freshly ground black pepper
    to taste
2 tsp. cornstarch dissolved in 1 tbs. cold
    water

Melt butter and sauté onion for 1 to 2 minutes, until softened. Pour in clam juice, add salt and pepper, and bring to a boil. Pour in a little of the cornstarch mixture and cook for 1 to 2 minutes, until mixture thickens. Add just enough cornstarch to bring sauce to a nice pouring consistency.

STEAMED TURKEY TENDERLOINS

Cooked turkey tenderloins make great sandwiches and salads. They steam in about 25 minutes and can be done ahead and refrigerated. A general rule is to steam for 15 minutes per 1-inch thickness. After the tenderloins have cooled, slice thinly and serve with Italian-Style Tuna Mayonnaise, *page 37, or* Italian Salsa Verde, *page 79, as part of a luncheon or salad buffet.*

2 turkey tenderloins, about 10–11 oz. each
kosher salt and freshly ground black pepper to taste

Place a rack in the bottom of the rice cooker container and add 3 cups of water. Season tenderloins with salt and pepper. Place tenderloins in one layer on a plate sprayed with non-stick spray. Cover plate with plastic wrap and place on rack in rice cooker container. Cover and steam tenderloins for about 25 minutes after water has come to a boil. Check after 20 minutes with an instant meat thermometer. Turkey should reach about 160°, and not be pink in the center. Remove from cooker and refrigerate if not serving immediately.

ITALIAN SALSA VERDE

This piquant green sauce is delicious on sliced cooked meats, plain pasta or rice. Make it at least an hour before serving so the flavors can combine. It keeps well refrigerated for several days, but bring to room temperature before serving.

2 loosely packed cups flat-leaf parsley leaves, (1 large bunch), washed and dried on paper towels
2 cloves garlic
2 canned anchovies, drained
2 tbs. capers, drained

⅓ cup extra virgin olive oil
1 tsp. Dijon-style mustard
2 tbs. grated Parmesan cheese
1 tbs. lemon juice
kosher salt and freshly ground black pepper to taste

Using the food processor, with the motor running, drop garlic in feed tube and process until chopped. Add parsley leaves and process until well chopped. Add remaining ingredients and process until well combined but not smooth. Pour into a small bowl, cover and allow to stand for 1 hour before using.

VEGETABLES FROM YOUR RICE COOKER

Steamed vegetables retain vitamins and other nutrients that are sometimes poured down the drain when vegetables are boiled. Steaming vegetables is quick and easy.

A stainless steel or plastic collapsible steamer basket makes a useful insert for the rice cooker to hold vegetables during the steaming process. If you are using a small rice cooker (3-cup capacity), a mini-steamer basket will fit. See pages 3–4 for a description of steamer racks.

We generally do not salt vegetables before steaming, but add seasonings to the cooked vegetables.

STEAMED ARTICHOKES

Steamed artichokes are a snap to do in the rice cooker. The size of your cooking container will limit the number of artichokes you can place in one layer and cook at the same time.

trimmed artichokes
3 cups water

Wash artichokes. Cut off artichoke stems and remove about 1 inch from top. Pull off 2 or 3 layers of outer leaves. Trim remaining uncut leaves straight across with scissors. Trim rough edges of artichoke bottom where leaves were removed.

Spray a steamer plate with nonstick spray. Add 3 cups of water to the rice cooker container and place artichokes on steamer plate (they do not have to stand on end). Cover and cook for about 35 to 45 minutes after water starts to steam, depending on size. Artichoke is done when bottom is easily pierced with a knife. If artichoke bottom is not tender, cover and let steam for a few more minutes. Remove artichokes from rice cooker and place on a serving platter.

Serve artichokes warm or at room temperature, and dip in mayonnaise, melted butter, or *Dijon Mustard Sauce,* page 113.

AROMATIC HERBED ARTICHOKES

Serve warm or cool with mayonnaise or Aioli, page 112. These make delicious picnic fare.

trimmed artichokes

FOR EACH ARTICHOKE, COMBINE

1 tbs. extra virgin olive oil	1 tbs. finely chopped fresh flat-leaf parsley
1 tsp. lemon juice	1/4 tsp. dried tarragon, or 1 tsp. chopped
2 tbs. dry white wine	fresh
1 tbs. finely minced onion	kosher salt and freshly ground black pepper

Wash artichokes and cut bottom stem flush with artichoke bottom. Cut about 1 inch off top of artichoke. Remove 2 or 3 layers of outer leaves; trim artichoke bottom. Pull out a few of the thorny center leaves and remove choke with a sharp spoon to make a small cup for olive oil herb mixture. Gently flatten artichoke to spread leaves slightly apart. Spoon olive oil herb mixture into spread leaves and center cup of artichoke.

Spray steamer plate with nonstick spray and add 3 cups water to the rice cooker container. Place artichokes stem-side down on steamer plate. Cover cooker and steam for about 35 to 45 minutes after water has come to a boil, depending on size of artichoke. Artichoke is done when bottom is easily pierced with a knife. Remove from container to serving plate.

BASIC STEAMED NEW POTATOES

Small new potatoes (1 to 2 inches diameter) cook beautifully in one layer in the rice cooker. A collapsible steamer basket works well for this, or use a steamer plate. Spray steamer plate with nonstick spray. Add scrubbed, unpeeled potatoes in one layer with 3 cups water. Cover and cook until potatoes are tender, about 20 minutes after water starts to boil. Test potatoes: if not completely cooked, replace cover and allow to steam for another few minutes. If all the water has evaporated, pour a small amount of water into cooking container for added steaming time. Serve hot with butter, salt and pepper; or with *Italian Salsa Verde*, page 79; *Aioli*, page 112; or use in one of the recipes that follow.

STEAMED NEW POTATOES WITH BUTTER AND PARSLEY

Melt 2 tbs. butter and combine with 1 tsp. lemon juice and 2 tbs. chopped fresh flat-leaf parsley. Pour over hot potatoes in serving bowl, toss to combine, and serve.

NEW POTATO SALAD

This is delicious as an accompaniment for grilled meats or paired with other salads on those nights when it is too hot to cook. Fresh tarragon or basil instead of thyme is a nice variation. The hot potatoes tend to be fragile so dress each layer as it is sliced.

2 tbs. extra virgin olive oil
2 tsp. sherry wine vinegar or rice wine
    vinegar
1/4 tsp. sugar
1 lb. *Basic Steamed New Potatoes,* page 84

leaves from two sprigs of fresh thyme
1 or 2 small green onions, white part with
    1 inch of green, minced
1 tbs. minced fresh flat-leaf parsley
kosher salt and freshly ground black pepper

Combine olive oil, wine vinegar and sugar. When potatoes are cool enough to handle, remove peel if desired and slice each potato into 1/2-inch thick slices. Place a layer of sliced potatoes in a small serving bowl and sprinkle with fresh thyme leaves, parsley, onions, salt and pepper. Drizzle with a small amount of olive oil mixture. Continue with another layer of potatoes, herbs and dressing until all potatoes and dressing have been used. Gently pour out dressing that has accumulated in bottom of bowl, and pour over salad again. Serve warm or at room temperature. If salad is refrigerated, allow it to warm a little before serving.

NEW POTATO WITH SMOKED SALMON SALAD

Servings: 4

Small new potatoes and smoked salmon dressed with dill and yogurt make a nice first course or luncheon salad.

12 oz. *Basic Steamed New Potatoes,* page 84, unpeeled
1 tbs. sweet-hot mustard
2 tbs plain yogurt
$\frac{1}{2}$ tsp. dried dill, or 1 tbs. chopped fresh
1 tbs. minced fresh flat-leaf parsley
kosher salt and freshly ground black pepper to taste
1–2 oz. thinly sliced smoked salmon, cut into 1-inch squares

When potatoes are cool enough to handle, slice each into quarters and place in a bowl. In a small bowl, mix together sweet-hot mustard, yogurt, dill and parsley. Gently toss with potatoes; season with salt and pepper to taste. Gently add smoked salmon pieces. Refrigerate until ready to serve. This can be made a day ahead.

STEAMED SWEET POTATOES

Steam sweet potatoes or yams in the rice cooker using a collapsible steamer basket. These are great served hot with a little butter, or purée them and make a Steamed Sweet Potato or Yam Pudding, *page 121.*

1 lb. sweet potatoes

Peel and cut potatoes into 1-inch cubes and place in a single layer in a steamer basket. Add 2 cups water to the rice cooker container, cover and bring to a boil. Carefully lower steamer basket into rice cooker. Cover and cook for about 17 minutes. Test for doneness with a fork. Remove from rice cooker and serve immediately.

SALAD NIÇOISE

The potatoes and green beans are steamed for this classic salad niçoise. Tuna packed in oil makes a big flavor difference.

1 lb. small *Steamed Green Beans,* page 98, stemmed
1 lb. *Basic Steamed New Potatoes,* page 84
1 tbs. unsalted butter
1 tbs. lemon juice
½ tsp. salt
2 cups water
2 tbs. capers, drained and rinsed
2 to 3 tbs. minced dried parsley or fresh flat-leaf
   parsley
2 fresh, ripe tomatoes, peeled, seeded and cut
   into quarters
2 hard boiled eggs, peeled, cut into quarters
about 20 olives, niçoise or kalamata
2 cans (6½ oz. each) white chunk tuna, well drained

NIÇOISE DRESSING

1/3 cup extra virgin olive oil
2 tbs. red wine vinegar
1 tsp. Dijon-style mustard
3 to 4 fresh thyme sprigs, leaves only
1 to 2 anchovies, finely chopped
salt and freshly ground black pepper to taste

Whisk dressing ingredients together in a small bowl to make an emulsion. Slice steamed potatoes into about 4 slices and layer in a mixing bowl. Sprinkle each layer with parsley and capers and drizzle with dressing. Coat cooked green beans with a little dressing.

To assemble: Use a large platter or assemble salads on individual plates. Place potatoes in the center of platter or divide among 3 to 4 plates. Arrange tomato wedges, eggs, green beans and olives around potatoes. Arrange drained tuna chunks around the salads. Drizzle vegetables and tuna with the dressing. Serve at room temperature.

STEAMED BUTTERNUT SQUASH

Look for ready-to-cook packages of butternut squash in the supermarket. Serve tossed with butter and seasoned with salt and pepper, or drizzled with maple syrup and a pinch of cinnamon.

1 lb. butternut squash, peeled, cut into 1-inch cubes

Place squash in a steamer basket. Add 2 cups water to the rice cooker container, cover and bring to a boil. Add steamer basket to cooker, cover, and cook for 10 to 12 minutes, until squash is tender. Remove from cooker, season as desired, and serve.

SWEET CORN

Sweet corn steams to perfection in the rice cooker.

fresh corn, trimmed

Remove cornhusks and silk and trim as needed. Spray a rice cooker steamer plate with non-stick cooking spray. Place corn ears on steamer plate. Add 1½ cups water to the rice cooker container, cover and bring to a boil. Carefully add steamer plate with corn to rice cooker, cover and cook for 10 minutes. Remove corn immediately. Season as desired and serve hot.

STEAMED BROCCOLI

Broccoli comes out of the rice cooker a pretty green color. Cook it to the texture you like.

broccoli

Spray a rice cooker steamer plate with nonstick cooking spray. Cut broccoli into florets or pieces with 2 to 3 inch stems. Place on steamer plate (or use a collapsible steamer basket and no steamer plate). Add 1½ cups water to rice cooker container, cover and bring to a boil. Place steamer plate with broccoli in rice cooker and cook for about 8 to 10 minutes, to desired crispness. Test with the tip of a knife. Remove to a serving dish. Season with salt, pepper, and a drizzle of extra virgin olive oil, if desired.

STEAMED CAULIFLOWER

Both whole heads and cauliflower florets steam well. After 1½ cups water come to a boil in the rice cooker, allow about 15 minutes to steam a small whole head, and 5 to 8 minutes for florets. Test for doneness with the tip of a knife.

BROCCOLI ASIAN-STYLE

Here is a delicious variation on plain steamed broccoli.

1 bunch broccoli, 1–1$\frac{1}{2}$ lbs.
2 tbs. vegetable oil
1 tbs. soy sauce
$\frac{1}{4}$–$\frac{1}{2}$ tsp. sambal oelek (a mixture of chiles, brown sugar and salt) or chile paste with garlic
1 tsp. toasted sesame oil

Cut broccoli into florets or pieces with 2-inch stems. In a shallow dish , combine oil, soy sauce, and sambal oelek. Add broccoli pieces and toss to coat with oil mixture. Spray rice cooker steamer plate or basket with nonstick spray. Add 1$\frac{1}{2}$ cups water to rice cooker, cover and bring to a boil. Carefully add steamer plate with broccoli. Cover rice cooker and steam for about 8 to 10 minutes, or until broccoli is cooked to desired texture. Remove to serving dish, drizzle with sesame oil and serve warm or at room temperature.

STEAMED ASPARAGUS

Asparagus keeps its bright green color when done in the rice cooker. If you have time, peel the stems for more tender spears.

1 lb. asparagus, stems trimmed

Spray a rice cooker steamer plate with nonstick cooking spray. Arrange asparagus on steamer plate. Pour ¾ cup water into the rice cooker container, cover and bring to a boil. Carefully add steamer plate to rice cooker and steam for about 8 minutes or until asparagus is cooked to desired tenderness. Remove asparagus spears immediately. If you are serving the asparagus as a hot vegetable, dress with a little butter, salt and pepper, and serve immediately. For use in a salad, run cold water over cooked spears, place on paper towels and pat dry before adding salad dressing.

VARIATION: **Asparagus with Zesty Lemon Topping:** Melt 2 tbs. unsalted butter in a small skillet. When foaming add ½ cup fresh bread crumbs and cook over medium heat until they start to brown. Quickly add grated zest of 1 lemon and 1 tsp. lemon juice. Pour over steamed asparagus and serve immediately.

MARINATED ASPARAGUS

Cooked asparagus with a light orange, ginger and soy sauce dressing makes a nice salad or side dish. Marinate asparagus while it is still a little warm to fully absorb dressing flavors.

1 lb. *Steamed Asparagus*, page 93
1 tbs. extra virgin olive oil
2 tsp. rice wine vinegar
1 tsp. toasted sesame oil
1 tbs. soy sauce
¼ tsp. sugar
½ tsp. grated orange rind
½ tsp. grated fresh ginger
1 tbs. orange juice
kosher salt and freshly ground black pepper

Dry steamed asparagus spears on paper towels, place in a shallow serving bowl. Combine remaining ingredients and pour over asparagus, turning spears until they are well coated with dressing. Serve at room temperature.

MARINATED MUSHROOMS

These piquant mushrooms keep well in the refrigerator for a few days and are a delicious addition to an antipasto or salad plate.

½ lb. button mushrooms
2 tbs. extra virgin olive oil
1 tbs. lemon juice
¼ cup rice wine vinegar
¼ cup dry sherry or white wine
1 clove garlic

¼ tsp. sugar
½ tsp. dried thyme
½ tsp. dried basil
generous dash crushed red pepper flakes
kosher salt and freshly ground black pepper
   to taste

Clean mushrooms and cut stems flush with mushroom top. If mushrooms are large, cut into quarters. Add all ingredients except mushrooms to the rice cooker container. Cover and bring to a boil. Add mushrooms to boiling liquid and cook for 5 minutes. Turn off cooker and let mushrooms cool in liquid. Season to taste with salt and pepper.

SUGAR SNAP PEAS

Crisp sugar snap peas cook beautifully in the rice cooker. Use a collapsible steamer basket to hold them.

1 lb. sugar snap peas, stemmed
$\frac{1}{2}$ tsp. toasted sesame oil

Add 1 cup water to rice cooker container, cover and bring water to a boil. Place steamer basket with sugar snap peas into cooker, cover and cook for about 4 to 5 minutes. Pour peas into a bowl, toss with sesame oil, salt and pepper and serve.

ORANGE GINGERED CARROTS

Servings: 2–3

Carrots flavored with fresh ginger and orange are a colorful and delicious addition to any meal. If you like crisp-tender carrots, remove them when they reach the desired degree of doneness. These can also be served at room temperature.

$^1/_2$ lb. carrots, peeled, sliced or cut into $^3/_8$-inch square by x 3-inch-long strips
grated zest of 1 orange
$^1/_2$ cup orange juice or combination orange juice and water
2 slices fresh ginger
1 tbs. butter

Add carrots and remaining ingredients to the rice cooker container. Cover and cook for 10 minutes after liquid has come to a boil. Check to see if carrots are tender. If not, cover and continue to cook for 1 to 2 minutes more, adding more water if needed. Remove from pan and serve.

GREEN BEANS

Green beans have a nice texture when steamed in the rice cooker. A collapsible steamer basket is great for holding beans. Use steamed beans in Salad Niçoise, *page 88, or other salads.*

1 lb. green beans, stemmed

Place beans in a steamer basket. Add 2 cups of water to the rice cooker container, cover and bring to a boil. Carefully add beans to rice cooker container and cook for 10 to 12 minutes. Check to see if beans are tender. If not, continue to steam for 1 to 2 minutes longer. Carefully remove lid, place beans on platter, season with salt, pepper and butter, and serve immediately, or allow to cool for use in another recipe.

ITALIAN ROMANO BEANS

Flat green Italian beans are delicious steamed and retain a firmer texture than when boiled. Cook in the same way as *Green Beans.*

GREEN BEAN AND MUSHROOM SAUTÉ

Servings: 2–3

After you have steamed tender young green beans, add a few mushrooms and green onions to make a tasty side dish.

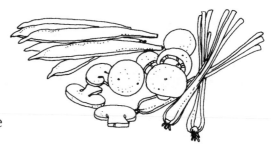

½ lb. green beans, stemmed and cooked, page 98
2 tbs. extra virgin olive oil
3–4 green onions, thinly sliced
5–6 medium mushrooms, thinly sliced
1 clove garlic, minced
1 tbs. cider vinegar
kosher salt and freshly ground black pepper to taste
2 tbs. diced roasted red pepper

Heat oil in a medium nonstick skillet and sauté onions and mushrooms over medium heat until mushrooms are soft. Add garlic and cook for another minute. Stir in cider vinegar; add salt, pepper, green beans and red pepper. Cook, stirring, for 1 to 2 minutes to heat beans.

Serve immediately, or refrigerate and serve at room temperature on a lettuce leaf as a salad.

BRAISED LEEKS

Young, small leeks about 1 inch in diameter are braised in vermouth and served with a mustard vinaigrette. Serve at room temperature on the buffet table or as a side dish for grilled meats.

4 to 6 small leeks, about 1- to 1¹/₂-inch
   diameter
1¹/₂ cups water

1 cup dry vermouth
1 large clove garlic, smashed
2 sprigs flat-leaf parsley

Cut off all but about 1 inch of green leek top, to make leeks about 5 or 6 inches in length. Cut lengthwise down center to within 1 inch of root. Trim bottom of root, leaving it intact to hold leek together. Carefully spread leek leaves and wash under running water to remove sand. Add leeks and remaining ingredients to rice cooker container. Cover and cook for about 18 to 20 minutes after water has come to a boil. Pierce leeks with a knife to see if they are tender. Remove from cooker and place in a shallow bowl. Pour 2 to 3 tbs. *Easy Mustard Vinaigrette,* page 114, over, turning leeks to coat all sides. Allow to cool and serve at room temperature.

STEAMED BEETS

Vivid red beets are steamed in an orange-flavored liquid that is then reduced to make a quick sauce. The beet skins slip off easily after cooking. An all-purpose stainless steel or plastic steamer basket works well to hold the beets.

5–6 beets, about 2 inches in diameter
grated zest and juice of 1 orange
1 tbs. rice wine vinegar

$\frac{1}{2}$ tsp. sugar
kosher salt and freshly ground black pepper
to taste

Cut off leafy beet tops to within 1 inch of beet. Wash, taking care not to break beet skin. Spray steamer basket with nonstick spray. Arrange beets in steamer; add 2$\frac{1}{2}$ cups water, orange zest and juice. Cover and cook for about 35 to 40 minutes, depending on size of beet. When beets are tender, remove to a plate and allow to cool. Peel, cut off tops and root ends, and slice.

Add rice wine vinegar, sugar, salt and pepper to rice cooker and continue to cook for about 8 to 10 minutes, reducing liquid to $\frac{1}{3}$ cup. Taste for seasoning and add a little more vinegar if desired. Pour sauce over beets and serve warm.

RED PEPPER AND MUSHROOM RISOTTO

Bring the chicken stock to a boil and keep it very hot while you are adding it to the rice.

3 tbs. extra virgin olive oil
1/2 cup chopped onion
1 cup coarsely chopped mushrooms
1/2 cup diced red pepper, peeled and seeded
1 cup Arborio or short-grain rice
3–3 1/4 cups chicken broth, see page 12

1 tbs. dried parsley
1/2 cup diced ham or Canadian bacon
1 dash crushed red pepper flakes
kosher salt and freshly ground black pepper
   to taste
1/2 cup grated Parmesan cheese

Bring chicken broth to a boil in the microwave or on the stovetop. Heat oil in the rice cooker container. Add onion and cook for 3 to 4 minutes, stirring, until onion softens. Add mushrooms and red pepper and cook for 3 to 4 minutes. Stir in rice and cook for 2 minutes, until rice is well coated. Add parsley, ham, red pepper flakes, salt and pepper. Slowly add hot chicken broth about 1/3 cup at a time to rice. Stir constantly, waiting until rice absorbs most of liquid before adding more stock. In about 15 to 18 minutes taste a rice grain to see if it is cooked through with no hard core. Spoon into a warm serving bowl, toss with Parmesan cheese and serve immediately.

Optional: Stir in 1 or 2 tbs. cold unsalted butter just before adding grated cheese.

SUMMER SQUASH

Yellow or green squash are flavored with some chopped basil and chives and steamed until tender. Use a collapsible steamer basket to hold the squash slices.

3–4 yellow squash or small green zucchini, cut into ¼-inch slices
1 tbs. olive oil
6–8 leaves fresh basil, cut into slivers
1 tsp. minced chives, or ½ tsp. dried
kosher salt and freshly ground black pepper to taste

Toss squash slices with oil, basil, chives, salt and pepper and place in a steamer basket. Add 1½ cups water to rice cooker container, cover, and bring to a boil. Carefully lower steamer basket with squash into cooker, cover and steam for about 8 to 10 minutes until squash is the desired tenderness. Do not overcook. Season to taste with salt and pepper, and drizzle with a little more olive oil.

WILD RICE

Wild rice isn't really a rice at all, but a grass that grows in the U.S. and Canada in an area surrounding the upper Great Lakes. Wild rice has a delicious nutty flavor and chewy texture. Formerly wild rice was very expensive, but it has become more reasonably priced with the cultivation of large fields in California. Wild rice adds an interesting texture and distinctive taste when served as a side dish or combined with other ingredients.

BASIC COOKED WILD RICE
Yield: 3 to 3½ cups cooked rice

Cooking time of wild rice varies widely depending upon how much of the bran has been removed during processing. Rely on the package instructions, or if you have purchased bulk wild rice, a general rule is that the darker (almost black) rice may take almost 1 hour to cook. Brown hued wild rice may be done in a little more than one-half hour, and light brown or "blonde" rice may cook in as little as 15 minutes.

1 cup wild rice
3½ to 4 cups chicken broth, see page 12, or water
½ tsp. salt

Place rice in a sieve and rinse well under running water. Add to the rice cooker container with salt. Rice can be cooked in either broth or water. We prefer a light chicken or vegetable broth. If you are using a salted broth, reduce or eliminate salt. Start with 4 cups of liquid for the darker colored rices, and a little less for the brown ones. Turn on the rice cooker, cover and allow to cook for about ½ to ⅔ of expected cooking time. Carefully open cooker and look at grains. When grains have started to "bloom," showing a little white on the ends, rice is almost cooked. Taste a grain. If rice still has a slight crunch, re-cover rice cooker and allow to cook for another 10 minutes.

Test again. When most of the grains have bloomed and grains are tender but still a little chewy, turn off rice cooker and allow rice to steam for a few minutes.

Cool and use as directed in the following recipes, or place in a container, cover and store in the refrigerator for up to 2 weeks, or freeze.

WILD RICE AND RAISIN TIMBALES

Makes 4–6 timbales

These savory molds are a delicious accompaniment for a holiday roast turkey or ham. Or serve them with roast chicken or pork. Substitute chopped dried apricots for the raisins for an interesting variation.

2 tbs. unsalted butter
$\frac{1}{2}$ cup chopped onion
$1\frac{1}{2}$ cups *Basic Cooked Wild Rice,* page 104
$\frac{1}{2}$ cup white raisins
2 large eggs
$\frac{1}{4}$ cup heavy cream
1 tsp. Worcestershire sauce
$\frac{1}{4}$ tsp. thyme
1 tbs. dried parsley, or 2 tbs. chopped fresh flat-leaf parsley
kosher salt and freshly ground black pepper to taste

Melt butter in a small nonstick skillet. Sauté onions for 5 to 6 minutes until soft, and set aside to cool slightly. In a medium bowl, beat eggs and cream; add Worcestershire, thyme, parsley, salt and pepper. Fold in wild rice, raisins and cooked onions.

Spray four 5- to 6-oz. custard cups or six 4-oz. timbales with nonstick spray. Fill molds about ¾ full of rice mixture. Cover each mold with foil, crimping foil securely at top of mold. Add about 2½ cups water to rice cooker; place molds on steamer plate. Cover rice cooker and turn on. Steam 5- to 6-oz. molds for about 20 minutes after water comes to a boil; small molds should be steamed for about 15 to 18 minutes. Timbales are done when a knife tip inserted into the center of the mold comes out clean.

Carefully remove molds from cooker with kitchen tongs. Allow to stand about 5 minutes before uncovering and un-molding. To un-mold, run a sharp knife blade around edge of timbale, place a plate upside down on top of timbale and invert. The timbale will release easily.

WILD RICE FRITTATA

Wild rice adds an interesting flavor and texture to the Italian-style egg frittata. If not using an ovenproof nonstick skillet, be sure to generously spray the skillet with nonstick spray for easier removal of the frittata from the pan.

2 small dried black shiitake mushrooms
2 tbs. extra virgin olive oil
5–6 green onions, white part with 1 inch of green, thinly sliced
4 large eggs
1 cup *Basic Cooked Wild Rice,* page 104
1 medium tomato, peeled, seeded, chopped
2 tbs. Parmesan cheese
1/4 tsp. dried tarragon
1 tsp. Worcestershire sauce
kosher salt and freshly ground black pepper to taste
additional Parmesan cheese for topping

Preheat oven to 400°. Cover dried mushrooms with boiling water and allow to stand for 10 to 15 minutes to soften. Remove from water, squeeze very dry, and cut out tough stems and discard. Cut mushroom caps into slivers.

Heat 1 tbs. olive oil in a 7- to 8-inch nonstick ovenproof skillet. Sauté onions and mushroom slivers for 2 to 3 minutes to soften. Place mushrooms and onions on a small plate and reserve. In a medium bowl, lightly beat eggs with a fork. Add onions, mushrooms and remaining ingredients to egg mixture. Spray skillet with nonstick spray and add remaining tbs. olive oil. Place skillet over medium heat, and when oil is hot, swirl it around sides of skillet and pour in egg mixture. Cook until eggs start to set, lifting up mixture at sides of pan so uncooked portion flows under cooked egg. When most of mixture has set, sprinkle with Parmesan cheese and place in a preheated oven. Bake for about 12 to 15 minutes, until center has puffed and mixture is firm to the touch. Remove from oven, run a spatula under frittata and slide it out of pan onto a plate lined with paper towels to absorb excess oil. Slide onto a warm serving plate and cut into wedges. Serve warm or at room temperature.

WILD RICE PANCAKES

Serve these for breakfast with a maple or fruit syrup, Dried Fruit Compote, *page 120, or top with creamed chicken or turkey to make a substantial lunch or brunch dish.*

3 large eggs, yolks separated
$3/4$ cup milk
2 tbs. melted unsalted butter
$1/3$ cup flour
$3/4$ tsp. kosher salt, or $1/2$ tsp. regular salt
$3/4$ cup *Basic Cooked Wild Rice,* page 104
$1/3$ cup cooked crumbled bacon pieces

Preheat griddle. Separate eggs. Place egg yolks in a medium bowl and beat until well combined. Stir in milk, butter, flour and salt. Add wild rice. In a separate bowl, beat egg whites until stiff but not dry. Gently fold egg whites and bacon into rice mixture. Cook pancakes on lightly oiled griddle until set and lightly browned. Turn and cook on the second side. Serve immediately.

WILD RICE AND MANGO SALAD

Serve this festive salad as a side dish for a holiday or fall dinner. For a variation, substitute chopped orange segments or ¹/₂ cup dried cranberries for the mango.

3 cups cooked wild rice

3 green onions, white part with 1 inch of green, minced

¹/₂ cup toasted chopped pecans

1 medium mango, peeled, cut into ¹/₂-inch chunks

VINAIGRETTE

2 tbs. extra virgin olive oil

zest of 1 orange

1 tbs. orange juice

1 tbs. cider vinegar

2 tsp. sugar

¹/₂ tsp. toasted sesame oil

kosher salt and freshly ground black pepper to taste

In a medium bowl, combine rice, onions, pecans and mango. In a small bowl, whisk together vinaigrette ingredients. Pour dressing over rice and toss to combine. Make 1 hour ahead to allow flavors to develop. Serve at room temperature.

AÏOLI

This garlicky, full-flavored mayonnaise is the perfect accompaniment for almost any vegetable. Prepare a platter of the best fresh vegetables: steamed tiny new potatoes, tender sweet corn, thin or fat asparagus spears, artichokes, broccoli and cauliflower florets, little green beans. Add some crunchy carrot sticks, red pepper rings, tomatoes, and any other favorites. Serve with steamed shrimp or poached salmon if you want to be more elaborate; with just bread sticks, you have great summer afternoon or evening party food.

4 to 5 cloves garlic	2 tsp. lemon juice
1/2 tsp. kosher or coarse sea salt	2 tbs. extra virgin olive oil
1 cup prepared mayonnaise	1/8 tsp. white pepper

Coarsely chop garlic and place in a mortar with salt. Crush garlic with pestle until very smooth. If you have a large mortar, add mayonnaise, lemon juice, olive oil and pepper to garlic and mix until well combined. If not using a mortar, chop garlic with salt, making a paste. Scrape garlic into a small bowl, add remaining ingredients and whisk until well combined. Refrigerate if not using immediately.

DIJON MUSTARD SAUCE

Here is a piquant mustard sauce that makes a great topping for steamed vegetables and also is a delicious dip for artichokes. Double the recipe if you wish.

¼ cup prepared mayonnaise
2 tbs. Dijon-style mustard
2 tbs. milk
freshly ground black pepper to taste
½ tsp. sugar
¼ tsp. dried tarragon, or 1 tsp. minced fresh

Combine ingredients in a small bowl and stir until smooth and blended. Refrigerate if not serving immediately.

EASY MUSTARD VINAIGRETTE

This zesty vinaigrette is great on Braised Leeks, *page 100, or any other vegetable to be served as an antipasto.*

¼ cup extra virgin olive oil
2 tbs. red wine vinegar
2 tsp. Dijon-style mustard
kosher salt and freshly ground black pepper

Whisk ingredients together in a small bowl until mixture forms an emulsion. Pour over cooked, drained vegetables. Allow vegetables to cool in vinaigrette or cover and refrigerate until ready to serve.

DESSERTS

For dessert, cook fresh summer fruits or steam puddings in the rice cooker. We have included a recipe for a *Sweet Potato Pudding* with pumpkin pie spices. The rice cooker makes custards easily, and we offer two, *Coconut Custard Flan* and a *Lemon Custard*. We have included a dried fruit compote made in the rice cooker that is excellent when served over ice cream or a simple cake.

STEAMED PEACHES

Fresh peaches are steamed with a little brown sugar and cinnamon for a simple delicious summer dessert.

2 large ripe peaches, peeled and pitted
2 tbs. brown sugar
$1/2$ tsp. cinnamon

Cut peaches into quarters. Place in a shallow dish that will fit inside rice cooker container with $1/2$-inch clearance around edges for steam to circulate. Sprinkle peaches with brown sugar and cinnamon.

Pour 1 cup water into rice cooker container and place a platform or rack to support dish in bottom of container. Place dish with peaches on rack, cover rice cooker and, after water comes to a boil, steam for about 5 to 7 minutes. Check at 5 minutes with the tip of a knife to see if peaches are tender. Carefully remove dish from rice cooker with a plate lifter and allow to cool. Serve at room temperature with a dollop of whipped cream or chill until ready to serve.

PEACHES WITH RASPBERRIES

Ripe peaches and raspberries are steamed together to make a picture-perfect dessert. Serve over vanilla ice cream or with a little whipped cream.

2 large, ripe peaches, peeled, cut in half and pitted
12–15 fresh raspberries
1 tbs. sugar
2 tbs. Triple Sec or raspberry liqueur
2 tsp. lemon juice

Place 4 peach halves cut-side up in a shallow dish that will fit inside rice cooker container with ½-inch clearance. Sprinkle fresh raspberries over peaches and top with sugar, liqueur and lemon juice.

Pour 1 cup water into the rice cooker container. Place a small platform in bottom of rice cooker. Place dish containing peaches on rack. Cover rice cooker and cook for about 10 minutes after water has come to a boil. Check at 8 minutes with the tip of a knife to see if peaches are tender. Do not overcook. Carefully remove dish from rice cooker with a plate lifter and allow to cool before serving. Serve with whipped cream or a scoop of ice cream.

POACHED APPLES

Use the rice cooker to make poached apples flavored with apple juice and cinnamon. Serve these for breakfast or as a light dessert with frozen yogurt.

3 cups apple juice
¼ cup sugar
1 tbs. lemon juice
1 slice of fresh ginger
1 cinnamon stick
3–4 cooking apples, such as Golden Delicious, peeled, cored, cut into quarters

Add all ingredients except apples to the rice cooker container. Cover and bring to a boil so sugar dissolves; continue to cook for 3 to 4 minutes while preparing apples. Add peeled apples to liquid, cover and cook for about 10 minutes, or until apples are tender when pierced with a knife. Turn off rice cooker and carefully remove cover. Lift out cooker container and place on a rack to cool. Remove apples and liquid to a serving dish, place in refrigerator and chill until ready to serve.

WINE-POACHED PEARS

Riesling or other white wine makes a good poaching liquid for pears. Bosc, Anjou or Bartlett pears work well for poaching. The poaching liquid can be reduced a little and served with the chilled pears.

4 medium pears, firm but ripe
2 cups white wine
$\frac{1}{2}$ cup sugar
$\frac{1}{2}$ tsp. vanilla

Peel pears and remove core from bottom. Cut a slice from bottom of each pear to form a flat base. Leave stem on top of pear. Place pears on a small flat plate and place in the bottom of the rice cooker container. Add white wine and sugar. Cover and start rice cooker. Check pears with the tip of a knife at 20 minutes and continue to cook for another 2 to 3 minutes if knife blade does not easily pierce pear. Remove plate from cooker with a plate lifter. Continue to cook liquid in rice cooker, uncovered, for another 6 to 7 minutes to reduce. When pears are cool enough to handle, move them to a bowl. Add vanilla to liquid and pour over pears. Chill for 1 to 2 hours or overnight in the refrigerator.

DRIED FRUIT COMPOTE

Packages of dried mixed fruit cooked in the rice cooker with a little orange juice and water make a healthful and easy dessert or dessert topping. Serve this over yogurt or ice cream, or on its own for brunch or lunch. Any combination of dried fruits can be used.

1 pkg. (7 oz.) dried mixed fruit, about 1½ cups
grated zest and juice of 1 orange
1 tbs. lemon juice
1 pinch kosher salt
½ tsp. vanilla, optional

Cut larger pieces of fruit into spoon-sized pieces. Place fruit in the rice cooker container with orange zest. Add enough water to orange juice to make 2 cups liquid. Add lemon juice and salt. Cover, bring liquid to a boil and cook for 10 minutes. Carefully check after 5 minutes and add a little more water if necessary. Check to see if fruit is tender after 10 minutes. If not, add a little more water and cook for 2 to 3 minutes longer.

Turn off rice cooker and pour fruit compote into a bowl. Add vanilla and allow fruit to cool to room temperature, or refrigerate and serve cold.

STEAMED SWEET POTATO PUDDINGS

Servings: 4

These puddings have a wonderful pumpkin pie flavor. Serve with a dollop of sweetened whipped cream. See Steamed Sweet Potatoes, *page 87.*

1¼ cups cooked, puréed sweet potato
   (about 1 lb. raw)
⅓ cup sugar
½ cup half-and-half or light cream
2 large eggs

½ tsp. cinnamon
¼ tsp. nutmeg
¼ tsp. powdered dried ginger
1 pinch powdered cloves
1 pinch kosher salt

Purée cooked sweet potato in the food processor. Add remaining ingredients and process until smooth. Spray four 5- to 6-oz. custard cups with nonstick cooking spray. Fill about ¾ full with pudding mixture. Cover each cup with a foil cap, crimping foil close to top of cup. Place 2 cups water in the rice cooker container with a steamer plate. Arrange custard cups on plate and cover. After water has come to a boil, cook for 20 minutes. If using smaller cups, cook for 15 to 18 minutes. Remove cups from cooker with kitchen tongs and allow to stand for 5 minutes before uncovering. These are best served at room temperature or slightly chilled.

STEAMED RHUBARB AND STRAWBERRIES

Strawberries and rhubarb are a classic combination. Steam them in the rice cooker and chill. Eat as a light dessert or serve on French toast or waffles for breakfast.

$1/2$ lb. rhubarb, trimmed and cut into 1-inch pieces
$1/2$ lb. strawberries, stemmed and quartered
$1/2$ cup sugar

Combine rhubarb, strawberries and sugar in a 7- to 8-inch stainless steel or deep glass dish for steaming. Pour 2 cups water into the rice cooker container. Place a steamer plate or small rack in bottom of rice cooker container and place dish with rhubarb and strawberries on rack.

After water has come to a boil, steam rhubarb for 10 to 12 minutes. Carefully remove the lid and check to see if rhubarb is soft; if not, steam for another 2 to 3 minutes. When rhubarb is soft, carefully remove bowl from steamer and allow to cool.

LEMON CUSTARD

Serve this lemony dessert with fresh berries or Steamed Rhubarb and Strawberries, *page 122.*

1 cup heavy cream
1/4 cup sugar
1 dash salt

2 large eggs plus 2 egg yolks
1/2 tsp. vanilla extract
1/2 tsp. lemon extract

Combine cream and sugar; beat until sugar dissolves. Add remaining ingredients and mix well. Spray four 6-oz. custard cups with nonstick cooking spray. Pour custard mixture through a sieve into custard cups. Cover each cup with a small piece of aluminum foil, crimping foil around top of cup. Add about 3 cups water to rice cooker container with a steaming rack in bottom of cooker. Place custard cups on rack. Cover and allow to steam for about 20 minutes after water has come to a boil. Check one cup by carefully removing from rice cooker with tongs. If the mixture is not fairly firm to touch, re-cover cup with foil and return to rice cooker for 2 to 3 minutes additional steaming. Remove from rice cooker and allow to stand for a few minutes before serving, or chill for a few hours.

Note: You can also pour mixture into a 3 1/2-cup ovenproof dish that will fit into cooker. Cover with foil. After water comes to a boil, steam for 25 to 30 minutes.

COCONUT CUSTARD FLAN

This creamy custard is filled with flaked coconut and has a brown sugar sauce.

⅓ cup sugar
1 cup heavy cream
¼ cup sugar
1 dash salt

2 large eggs plus 2 egg yolks
1 tsp. vanilla
⅛ tsp. almond extract
¼ cup sweetened dried flaked coconut

Place ⅓ cup sugar in a small nonstick skillet. Cook over medium heat until sugar melts and turns a deep shade of caramel. Warm a 3½-cup ovenproof dish so the hot caramel will not crack it. Make sure dish will fit into the rice cooker. Pour hot caramel into dish, tilting so sugar mixture covers bottom of dish. Lightly beat together heavy cream, sugar, and salt until sugar dissolves. Add remaining ingredients and mix well. Pour custard mixture on top of caramel. Add 3 to 4 cups water to rice cooker container. Cover custard dish with foil and place on rack above water in cooker. Cover cooker and cook for about 25 to 30 minutes after water comes to a boil. Check to see if mixture just jiggles slightly and is fairly firm. Carefully remove dish from rice cooker and allow to stand for a few minutes before un-molding, or chill in the refrigerator before un-molding and serving.

OTHER THINGS YOU CAN DO IN A RICE COOKER

See pages 3–4 for a description of steamer racks.

EGGS

Be sure to make a small hole with a pin on the rounded end of each egg shell before cooking to help keep eggs from cracking.

HARD-COOKED EGGS

Place eggs on a steamer plate or basket. Add 2 cups water to the rice cooker container, cover and bring to a boil. Carefully add steamer plate to rice cooker, cover and cook for 14 to 16 minutes. Remove eggs from cooker and place in bowl of cold water to cool.

SOFT-COOKED EGGS

Place eggs on a steamer plate or basket. Add ³/₄ cup water to the rice cooker container, cover and bring to a boil. Carefully add steamer plate to rice cooker, cover and cook for about 8 minutes. Remove eggs from cooker and serve hot.

POACHED EGGS

Spray small custard cups with nonstick cooking spray. Break one egg in each cup; season with salt and pepper; add a sliver of butter if desired. Bring 1 cup water to a boil in the rice cooker container. Add steamer plate with egg cups to rice cooker, cover and cook until eggs reach desired firmness. Soft eggs generally cook in 5 to 6 minutes; firmer eggs in 7 to 8 minutes. Carefully remove egg cups from steamer, run the thin blade of a knife around edge of cups, and slide eggs onto individual warm serving plates, or onto buttered toast. Serve immediately.

BRATWURST WITH SAUERKRAUT

Servings: 4

Serve these on a bun and slather with mustard. Prepared bacon bits work well here.

1 can (14 oz.) sauerkraut, rinsed with cold water and drained
½ cup chopped onion
1 cup beer
1 cup chicken broth, see page 12

2 slices crumbled cooked bacon
3 to 4 juniper berries, optional
1 bay leaf
½ tsp. dried thyme
4 bratwurst or other cooked sausages

Place all ingredients except bratwurst in the rice cooker container. After liquid has come to a boil, cook for 15 minutes. Carefully remove cover, add sausages and continue to cook for another 5 to 7 minutes, until sausages are plump and heated through. Turn off rice cooker and serve.

BRATWURST OR SMOKED SAUSAGES STEAMED IN BEER

Any cooked sausages heat easily in the rice cooker. Place sausages in the rice cooker container, add 1 cup full-flavored beer or ale, cover and cook for 8 to 10 minutes. When sausages are steaming, turn off cooker and remove to a serving platter. Serve with different kinds of mustard, potato salad, a crunchy vegetable tray and beer for a Monday night football party.

STEAMED GRAINS

Rice is only one of many interesting grains that can be cooked in the rice cooker. Barley and millet are nice alternatives to rice and can be used somewhat interchangeably with rice in stuffings and other preparations. Quinoa, too, is a delicious variation that is easily cooked in the rice cooker. It provides a nice foil for all the spices and herbs generally used with rice.

Millet looks and tastes a lot like a more substantial couscous. Use it instead of rice in your chili bowl; with a curry sauce; or with a jar of your favorite spaghetti sauce. Millet also makes a great stuffing for peppers or tomatoes— or add eggs and make fritters. Buy hulled millet because the un-hulled kind takes substantially longer to cook.

MILLET PARMESAN

The light fluffy millet grains can be compared to couscous in size and texture. Some good Parmesan cheese and a little butter folded into the cooked millet makes a terrific side dish that is similar to polenta and can be served with almost any entrée. When cooking millet, be sure to add either a little butter or oil so the grains remain separate when cooked.

1/2 cup uncooked hulled millet
1 3/4 cups chicken broth, see page 12, or water
3 tbs. unsalted butter, divided
kosher salt and freshly ground black pepper to taste
1/2 cup Parmesan cheese

Toast millet grains in a heavy skillet over medium heat for about 5 minutes, until millet starts to brown and smells lightly toasted. Add chicken broth, 1 tbs. of the butter and salt and pepper to the rice cooker container. Add toasted millet to rice cooker; cover and cook for about 40 minutes, until rice cooker turns off. Allow millet to steam for 10 minutes. Carefully remove cover and stir in remaining 2 tbs. butter and Parmesan cheese. Spoon into a warm serving bowl and serve immediately.

TOMATOES STUFFED WITH MILLET

Servings: 6

This is a colorful side dish to serve with grilled meats or as part of a light buffet. Millet makes a savory stuffing for almost any vegetable.

6 medium tomatoes
3 tbs. unsalted butter
1/4 cup diced onion
1 tsp. dried basil, or 3 tbs. chopped fresh
2 tbs. minced fresh flat-leaf parsley, or 1 tsp.
  dried
1/2 tsp. kosher salt
generous grinding black pepper to taste
1 1/2 cups *Millet Parmesan,* page 129, omitting
  butter and cheese
1/4 cup grated Parmesan cheese

Cut a ½-inch slice off top of tomatoes. Carefully cut around center of each tomato with a small knife, leaving a ½-inch shell. Remove centers with a small sharp spoon and chop coarsely. Rinse out tomatoes to remove seeds and sprinkle inside of each tomato shell with a little salt. Turn shells upside down on a plate to drain for 15 to 20 minutes. Heat butter in a small skillet and sauté onions for 5 to 6 minutes, until soft. Add basil, parsley, salt, pepper, cooked millet and chopped tomato pieces. Cook for 1 to 2 minutes. Stir in 2 tbs. of Parmesan cheese. Fill tomatoes with millet mixture, dot with a little butter and sprinkle with remaining Parmesan cheese.

Use a small plate that will fit into the rice cooker container with about ½-inch clearance for steam to circulate. Place stuffed tomatoes on plate. Place 1½ cups water in bottom of rice cooker container, cover and bring to a boil. Carefully place plate with tomatoes on a rack in rice cooker. Cover and time tomatoes to steam for about 5 to 6 minutes, just until tomatoes are heated all the way through. Carefully remove tomatoes to serving plates. Serve warm or at room temperature.

QUICK COOKED BARLEY

Use quick cooking "pearled" barley with some dried herbs and vegetables to make a hearty side dish, or use as a stuffing for peppers or tomatoes.

2 tbs. unsalted butter
2 tbs. dried onion pieces
2 tbs. dried parsley
1½ cups quick pearled barley
3¼ cups chicken broth, see page 12
½ cup water
salt and freshly ground black pepper to taste

Add all ingredients to the rice cooker container, cover and cook until rice cooker shuts off. Carefully remove cover and stir to loosen barley from bottom of pan. Re-cover and allow to steam for 5 minutes before serving.

GARDEN VEGETABLE BARLEY STEW

Fresh vegetables cooked with barley make a hearty lunch or supper. Serve with garlic bread.

2 cups diced eggplant
3 cups chicken broth, see page 12
1 cup quick-cooking pearled barley
2 tbs. unsalted butter
2 plum tomatoes, seeded and coarsely
 chopped
2 small zucchini, cut in half length-wise and
 sliced

1 large red bell pepper, cored and diced
1 large onion, cut in half and thinly sliced
2 cloves garlic, minced
1 tbs. dried parsley, or 3 tbs. chopped fresh
1 tsp. dried thyme
$\frac{1}{2}$ tsp. dried basil, or 2 tbs. chopped fresh
kosher salt and freshly ground black pepper
 to taste

Peel and dice eggplant and place in a microwavable dish. Microwave on HIGH for 2 minutes, uncovered. Pat dry with paper towels. Add eggplant and remaining ingredients to the rice cooker container. Cover and cook until rice cooker turns off, about 20 minutes. Carefully remove cover, stir, and re-cover. Allow to steam for 10 minutes before serving. Pass grated Parmesan cheese, if desired.

BARLEY AND SUN-DRIED TOMATO PILAF

Servings: 4 as a side dish

Barley makes an interesting substitute for rice in a pilaf, and the sun-dried tomatoes add a flavorful punch.

2 tbs. extra virgin olive oil
1/2 cup chopped onion
1 cup pearled barley
2 1/4 cups chicken broth, see page 12
1 tbs. dried parsley, or 2 tbs. chopped fresh
1/4 cup slivered sun-dried tomatoes
1/2 tsp. salt
freshly ground black pepper to taste
1 cup frozen green peas, defrosted

Heat olive oil in the rice cooker container. Sauté onion in oil for 2 to 3 minutes to soften; add barley and stir to coat with oil. Add all remaining ingredients except green peas. Cover and cook until rice cooker shuts off. Carefully remove cover, quickly stir mixture and add green peas. Cover and allow to steam for 10 minutes before serving. Serve immediately.

COMPANY OATMEAL

Servings: 4

This is a great treat for a cold winter morning or when you want a tasty breakfast for the children.

1⅓ cups Old Fashioned Quaker Oats (not quick cooking)
2 cups apple juice
¾ cup water
⅓ cup raisins
1 dash salt

Add ingredients to the rice cooker container. Stir and cover rice cooker. Turn on and cook oatmeal until rice cooker turns off. Stir once during cooking. After rice cooker shuts off, allow to steam for 10 minutes before serving.

QUINOA

Quinoa is a high-protein, natural, whole grain that cooks into a nutty, flavorful side dish. It can be used interchangeably with rice in many dishes, or cooked very simply with a few onion and parsley flakes.

1 cup quinoa, rinsed
2 cups water
1 tbs. unsalted butter or vegetable oil
kosher salt
1 tbs. dried minced onion
1 tbs. parsley flakes

Add quinoa, water, butter or oil, salt, dried onion and parsley flakes to the rice cooker container. Cover and cook until rice cooker shuts off. Carefully remove cover, stir and re-cover. Allow to steam for 10 minutes before serving.

For a variation, substitute chicken or beef broth, see page 12, for water. Use quinoa to stuff tomatoes or peppers.

CURRIED QUINOA PILAF

The mild curry flavor makes this a delicious accompaniment for grilled meats or vegetables. Top with toasted slivered almonds and fresh cilantro leaves just before serving.

2 tbs. unsalted butter
1 tsp. curry powder
1/2 cup chopped onions
1 clove garlic, minced
1/3 cup coarsely grated carrot
1/4 lb. fresh mushrooms, chopped
2 cups water
1 cup quinoa, rinsed and drained

kosher salt and freshly ground black pepper
   to taste
1/2 tsp. lemon zest
1 tbs. lemon juice
1/4 cup white or dark raisins
1/4 cup slivered toasted almonds and fresh
   cilantro leaves for garnish

Melt butter in the rice cooker container. Add curry powder and cook for 1 to 2 minutes to bring out curry flavor. Add onions, garlic, carrot and mushroom pieces. Cook, stirring, for 1 to 2 minutes. Add water, quinoa, salt, pepper, lemon zest and juice. Cover rice cooker and cook until it shuts off. Carefully remove cover, stir in raisins, re-cover and allow to steam for 10 minutes. Spoon into a serving dish and top with almonds and cilantro. Serve immediately.

SAVORY MUSHROOM TIMBALES

Vegetable custards make an easy, different vegetable preparation for those special dinners. They steam in about 20 minutes. Allow to stand for about 5 minutes, and then un-mold. Four 6-oz. custard cups are a tight fit side by side in a medium size rice cooker, but you can place one on top, supporting it with the rims of the three lower cups. If you use smaller cups or timbales, steam for 15 to 18 minutes.

2 tbs. unsalted butter
½ lb. mushrooms, coarsely chopped
2–3 tbs. minced shallots or green onions
1 tbs. dried parsley
1 tsp. dried chives
⅓ cup heavy cream
1 tsp. Worcestershire sauce
¼ tsp. dried tarragon
2 large eggs
kosher salt and freshly ground black pepper to taste

Melt butter in a small skillet. Sauté mushrooms for 3 to 4 minutes, until they soften and release their liquid. Add shallots, parsley and chives. Cook for another 1 to 2 minutes to soften shallots. Allow to cool slightly. Pour mushrooms into a food processor bowl with heavy cream and process until mixture is fairly smooth. Add Worcestershire, tarragon, eggs, salt and pepper. Pulse 7 to 8 times just to combine ingredients.

Spray custard cups or timbale molds with nonstick spray. Fill molds about ¾ full. Cover top of each mold with foil, crimping it near top of mold. Place molds on a steamer rack. Add about 3 cups water to cooker, cover, turn the rice cooker on and bring water to a boil. Carefully add steamer rack with timbales to rice cooker. Cover and steam for 20 minutes. Turn cooker off and carefully remove timbales with kitchen tongs. Check one custard with the tip of a knife to make sure filling has set. Allow to stand for about 5 minutes. Remove foil. Run a thin knife blade around edge of timbales. Place a plate upside down on top of each timbale and invert. The timbale will un-mold easily. Serve warm.

These reheat beautifully in the microwave, lightly covered with plastic wrap and cooked for 40 to 60 seconds on high power.

STEAMED CARROT AND ORANGE TIMBALES

Servings: 4

This pretty addition to any dinner plate assembles quickly if you have pre-cooked the carrots. Four 6-oz. custard cups are a tight fit side by side in a medium size rice cooker, but you can place one on top, supporting it with the rims of the three lower cups. If you use smaller cups or timbales, steam for 15 to 18 minutes.

2 tbs. unsalted butter
4 green onions, white part only, thinly
  sliced
2 cups cooked sliced carrots
grated zest of 1 orange
2 tbs. orange juice
2 tbs. heavy cream
2 large eggs
kosher salt and white pepper to taste

Melt butter in a small skillet. Sauté onions for 1 to 2 minutes to soften. Combine onions, cooked carrots, orange zest, orange juice and heavy cream in a food processor workbowl. Process until mixture is quite smooth. Add eggs, salt and pepper and pulse 7 to 8 times just to combine ingredients. Spray four 5- to 6-oz. custard cups or timbale molds with nonstick spray. Fill the molds about ¾ full and tightly cover each mold with foil. Crimp foil close to top of mold to avoid getting water into cup during the cooking process. Place timbales on a steamer rack. Pour about 3 cups water into the rice cooker container, cover and bring water to a boil. Carefully add steamer rack with molds to rice cooker container. Cover and steam for about 20 minutes.

Remove molds from water with kitchen tongs. Check one custard with the tip of a knife to make sure filling has set. Allow to stand for about 5 minutes before uncovering and un-molding. Run a thin knife blade around edge of timbale to loosen and then place a plate upside down over mold and invert. The timbale will un-mold easily. Serve warm.

These reheat beautifully in the microwave, lightly covered with plastic wrap and cooked for 40 to 60 seconds on high power.

DIM SUM DELIGHTS

The rice cooker makes a great steamer to reheat the Chinese steamed buns and filled wrappers that you find in the market or Chinese take-out counters. Recipes follow for a Chinese-style steamed bun filled with a quick barbecue chicken filling, a great shrimp and pork Shao Mai Dumpling, Pearl Balls, and steamed Chicken Treasure Packages in foil.

BARBECUED CHICKEN BUNS

Makes 8

Flavor some cooked chicken with your favorite barbecue sauce for a tasty filling for the Chinese-style steamed buns. The bun dough is easy to make in the food processor.

1 cup cake flour
1 cup all-purpose flour
2 tbs. sugar
2½ tsp. baking powder

1 tbs. vegetable shortening
⅔ cup milk
¾ cup cooked chicken, in ⅜-inch cubes
⅓ cup barbecue sauce

Add flours, sugar and baking powder to the food processor workbowl. Pulse 3 or 4 times to mix well. Add shortening and pulse several times to combine. With processor running, add milk and process until dough forms a ball. Turn out dough onto a lightly floured board and knead for 1 to 2 minutes. Dough will be quite soft. Form dough into a log about 12 inches long. Cover with plastic wrap and allow dough to rest while preparing filling.

Combine chicken pieces and barbecue sauce in a small saucepan. Heat through over low heat, stirring frequently so sauce doesn't stick or burn. Remove from heat and allow to cool before filling buns.

To form buns, cut dough into 8 equal pieces. Take a piece of dough and flatten into a 3- to 4-inch circle, thicker in the middle than on the edges. Put about 2 tbs. of filling in the middle of the circle and pull up sides of dough. Pleat and pinch dough to seal top. Place each bun on a 2-inch square of aluminum foil.

Place a small platform in the rice cooker container to hold the steamer plate about 2 inches above water. Add about 3 cups water to the rice cooker container, cover and bring water to a boil. Place 4 buns on steamer plate and, using a plate holder, carefully place plate on rack in rice cooker. Cover and steam for 10 minutes. Remove cooked buns with kitchen tongs and repeat steaming process with remaining 4 buns. These buns freeze well. Serve at room temperature or reheat by steaming over hot water for a few minutes.

SHAO MAI DUMPLINGS

A Cantonese dim sum is not complete without these tasty steamed dumplings. Purchase round 3-inch shao mai wrappers, or cut square won ton wrappers into 3-inch circles.

FILLING

1 dried shiitake mushroom

¼ lb. peeled, de-veined small raw shrimp

¼ lb. lean ground pork

2 tbs. peeled, finely diced water chestnut or jicama

2 green onions, white part with 1 inch of green, finely minced

1 tsp. grated fresh ginger

1 clove garlic, minced

1 tbs. oyster sauce or Worcestershire sauce

kosher salt and white pepper to taste

3-inch round shao mai wrappers

fresh cilantro leaves

SHAO MAI DIPPING SAUCE

3 tbs. soy sauce

2 tbs. rice wine vinegar

2 tsp. hot pepper oil

Cover dried mushroom with boiling water and let stand for 15 minutes to soften. Squeeze dry, cut out and discard the tough stem and finely chop the cap. If preparing by hand, all ingredients including shrimp should be finely chopped and then combined. If using the food processor, mince water chestnut, onions, ginger and garlic in food processor and then add remaining ingredients, pulsing a few times to chop fine. Do not over-process.

To assemble: Place about 1 tbs. of the mixture in center of a wrapper. Bring sides of wrapper up around filling, pleating wrapper at the edge to form a cup. The finished shao mai will look like a tiny cupcake showing meat filling in center. Place a fresh cilantro leaf over meat. Keep unused wrappers covered with a damp paper towel so they don't dry out.

To steam: Place about 2 cups water in the rice cooker container. Place a small platform or artichoke holder to hold the steamer plate in rice cooker container. Spray steamer plate with nonstick spray and arrange shao mai on plate about 1 inch apart. When water is steaming in rice cooker, carefully lower plate into rice cooker onto platform. Cover and steam for 15 minutes. Remove shao mai and serve immediately.

To serve: Pour a small amount of dipping sauce into small individual dishes. Dip shao mai into sauce. The cooked shao mai can be refrigerated and reheated in the microwave or steamed for a few minutes. These can also be assembled ahead, covered with plastic wrap and refrigerated a few hours before steaming. The recipe amounts can easily be doubled.

CHICKEN TREASURE PACKAGES

Makes 16 pieces

Tender pieces of chicken breast are marinated and then wrapped in foil and steamed. These succulent morsels can be made ahead, refrigerated and steamed just before serving. The recipe can be increased to meet demand.

2 boneless, skinless chicken breasts

MARINADE

1/2 tsp. grated fresh ginger

1 tbs. hoisin sauce

1 tbs. soy sauce

1 tbs. dry sherry or shao xing rice
   wine

1 tsp. toasted sesame oil

1 tsp. cornstarch

4 green onions, white part with 1
   inch of green, slivered

fresh cilantro leaves

16 pieces of foil, about 5 inches square

Cut each chicken breasts into 8 pieces. Combine marinade ingredients in a small bowl, add chicken pieces and marinate for 15 minutes.

To assemble: Place a drained piece of chicken just below the center of a foil square. Top with slivers of green onions and 2 to 3 fresh cilantro leaves. Bring top half of foil piece down over chicken even with bottom edge of foil. Fold up about 1/4-inch from bottom and then make a fold 1/4-inch in from each side. Continue to fold up bottom and side edges until you are close to the chicken piece inside foil.

Place 1 cup water in the rice cooker container and bring to a boil. Place foil packets on a collapsible steamer basket or rack, allowing room for steam to circulate around packets, and carefully lower into rice cooker. Cover and cook for 7 minutes. Remove packets from steamer and serve as an appetizer.

PORK PEARL BALLS

Remember to start soaking the rice about 3 hours before you start making these. Serve them with Shao Mai Dipping Sauce, *page 144. Leftovers can be refrigerated and re-steamed or reheated in the microwave the next day.*

½ cup short grain or Calrose rice
¼ lb. raw shrimp, peeled, de-veined
3–4 water chestnuts, diced finely, about ¼ cup
½ lb. lean ground pork
1 tbs. minced green onion, white part only
1 tsp. minced fresh ginger
2 tsp. soy sauce
½ tsp. toasted sesame oil
½ tsp. sugar
¼ tsp. kosher salt
1 pinch white pepper
1½ tbs. cornstarch
2 tsp. rice wine or dry sherry

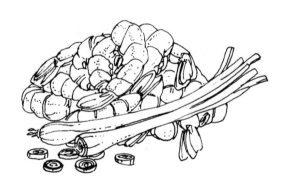

Place rice in a small bowl and rinse in several changes of cold water. Cover the rinsed rice with 1 cup water and allow to stand for 3 to 4 hours. Pour rice into a strainer and allow to drain for 30 minutes. Turn rice out on a sheet of waxed paper or a large plate. Place shrimp in a food processor workbowl and process to a smooth paste. Scrape down sides, add remaining ingredients and pulse to mix thoroughly. Refrigerate to firm up while rice soaks.

To assemble: Form about 2 tbs. of the pork and shrimp mixture into a ball. Roll formed balls into the drained rice to lightly coat surface with rice. Spray a plate that will fit into the rice cooker with nonstick cooking spray. Arrange rice-coated balls on plate, allowing a small space between balls. Pour about 2 cups of water into rice cooker container and place a small can or rack in bottom to hold the plate above water. Cover rice cooker and bring water to a boil. When water boils, carefully lower plate onto rack, cover and steam for 20 minutes. Remove balls from rice cooker and serve while hot with *Shao Mai Dipping Sauce,* page 144. These can be refrigerated and re-steamed in the rice cooker before serving.

DOLMAS (RICE-STUFFED GRAPE LEAVES)

These rice-stuffed grape leaves are wonderful served as party appetizers, lunches or picnic fare, and they keep well for several days in the refrigerator. Use leftover grape leaves to wrap around salmon or chicken before steaming or grilling.

5 tbs. extra virgin olive oil
½ cup finely chopped onion
1 clove garlic, minced
kosher salt and freshly ground black pepper
   to taste
½ lb. mushrooms, chopped

2 tbs. lemon juice
¾ cup cooked long-grain rice
½ tsp. dill weed
2 tbs. minced fresh flat-leaf parsley
2 tbs. pine nuts or chopped almonds
1 jar (8 oz.) grape leaves in brine

Heat 3 tbs. of the olive oil in a medium nonstick skillet and sauté onion for 3 to 4 minutes, until translucent. Increase heat and add garlic, salt, pepper, chopped mushrooms and lemon juice. Cook for 3 to 4 minutes, until mushrooms are tender. Stir in cooked rice, dill weed, parsley and pine nuts. Set aside and allow to cool.

Rinse grape leaves in cold water. Separate leaves, cut off long stems with scissors and pat dry with paper towels. Place leaves shiny-side down on a plate or board. To fill, place 1 tbs.

of the rice mixture near the stem end and roll up jelly-roll fashion, tucking in sides of leaves to make a neat package as you roll. (See illustration, below). If leaves are extra large, trim a little from sides so the wrapper doesn't overwhelm filling. If there is a tear in the leaf, patch with a piece of trimmed excess or a piece from another leaf.

Place dolmas in one layer on a plate that will fit into the rice cooker container. If necessary, cook dolmas in 2 batches. Add ¼ cup lemon juice, remaining 2 tbs. olive oil and 3 cups of water to rice cooker container. Liquid should come part way up sides of dolmas. Place another plate on top of dolmas, leaving a small space between plate and sides of cooker for steam to circulate. Cover rice cooker and cook for 20 minutes. Turn off cooker and remove cover. Allow to stand until plate is cool enough to lift out. Place warm dolmas on a plate. Serve warm, at room temperature or chilled.

INDEX

Serve Creative, Easy, Nutritious Meals with nitty gritty® Cookbooks

1 or 2, Cooking for
100 Dynamite Desserts
9 x 13 Pan Cookbook
Bagels, Best
Barbecue Cookbook
Beer and Good Food
Blender Drinks
Bread Baking
Bread Machine
Bread Machine II
Bread Machine III
Bread Machine V
Bread Machine VI
Bread Machine, Entrees
Burger Bible
Cappuccino/Espresso
Casseroles
Chicken, Unbeatable
Chile Peppers
Clay, Cooking in
Coffee and Tea
Convection Oven

Cook-Ahead Cookbook
Crockery Pot, Extra-Special
Deep Fryer
Dehydrator Cookbook
Edible Gifts
Edible Pockets
Fabulous Fiber Cookery
Fondue and Hot Dips
Fondue, New International
Fresh Vegetables
Freezer, 'Fridge, Pantry
Garlic Cookbook
Grains, Cooking with
Healthy Cooking on Run
Ice Cream Maker
Indoor Grill, Cooking on
Italian Recipes
Juicer Book II
Kids, Cooking with Your
Kids, Healthy Snacks for
Loaf Pan, Recipes for
Low-Carb Recipes

Lowfat American
No Salt No Sugar No Fat
Party Foods/Appetizers
Pasta Machine Cookbook
Pasta, Quick and Easy
Pinch of Time
Pizza, Best
Porcelain, Cooking in
Pressure Cooker, Recipes
Rice Cooker
Rotisserie Oven Cooking
Sandwich Maker
Simple Substitutions
Skillet, Sensational
Slow Cooking
Slow Cooker, Vegetarian
Soups and Stews
Soy & Tofu Recipes
Tapas Fantásticas
Toaster Oven Cookbook
Waffles & Pizzelles
Wraps and Roll-Ups

For a free catalog, call: Bristol Publishing Enterprises
(800) 346-4889
www.bristolpublishing.com